PROTECTING YOUR CHILD FROM SEXUAL ABUSE

WHAT YOU NEED TO KNOW TO KEEP YOUR KIDS SAFE

ELIZABETH JEGLIC, PHD
——————— and ———————
CYNTHIA CALKINS, PHD

Skyhorse Publishing

Skyhorse Publishing books may be purchased in bulk at special discounts for sales promotion, corporate gifts, fund-raising, or educational purposes. Special editions can also be created to specifications. For details, contact the Special Sales Department, Skyhorse Publishing, 307 West 36th Street, 11th Floor, New York, NY 10018 or info@skyhorsepublishing.com.

Skyhorse® and Skyhorse Publishing® are registered trademarks of Skyhorse Publishing, Inc.®, a Delaware corporation.

Visit our website at www.skyhorsepublishing.com.

10 9 8 7 6 5 4 3 2 1

Library of Congress Cataloging-in-Publication Data is available on file.

Cover design by Jane Sheppard
Cover photo credit: iStockphoto

Print ISBN: 978-1-5107-2868-4
Ebook ISBN: 978-1-5107-2869-1

Printed in the United States of America

Contents

Introduction

This book represents perhaps the most important endeavor that we have embarked on to date. Together we have written over one hundred journal articles, book chapters, and a book on sexual violence prevention. As professors of psychology, our goal has been to figure out ways to reduce rates of sexual violence in our society. As clinical psychologists, we have both worked directly with sexual offenders, trying to help them to reduce their risk of reoffense. And as researchers, we have devoted ourselves to addressing this problem on a larger scale, studying how we as a society might do better—through our policies, treatment programs, and societal norms—to lower rates of sexual violence. The majority of this work has been directed at other academics in our field, usually in the form of peer-reviewed research publications, or it has been through work with the offenders themselves. However, in the last decade we have both become mothers, and we began to think about sharing our work with a new audience—parents like ourselves. We have both struggled with reconciling what we know to be true based on the research (risks are lower than assumed) and what we feel as mothers (wanting to protect our children at all costs). Sexual violence prevention is not easy or simple, but research shows that there are things we *can* do. We think it is very important that parents are informed.

If you are reading this book, you are probably someone who likes to be kept aware, who strives to do the best they can for their children, and who understands the complexity of issues like sexual violence. As we thought about writing this book, one of the first questions we asked ourselves was: Will anyone read it? We had editors tell us: "This is a really important topic. But no one will read that book." It is for that precise reason that we felt compelled to write it. Sexual violence is a very real problem, and sticking our heads in the sand will not make it go away. We know, however, that there is an audience of educated and concerned parents who do want to learn more.

The topic of sexual violence makes some people very uncomfortable, and people tend to avoid what makes them uncomfortable. Whenever someone asks what we do or what we study and we reply that we do research on sex offenders, the conversation invariably stops there. We want to change that. As psychologists, we know that avoidance (i.e., pretending a problem doesn't exist) is a poor coping strategy. While it stops the anxiety in the short term, it doesn't solve the problem and often makes it hard to envision more proactive strategies for dealing with it. So we are thankful for readers like you who, just by picking up this book, are beginning to nudge our society toward more open dialogue around important issues like sexual violence.

Between the two of us, we have five children aged eight and under. We want to protect them and keep them safe at all costs. As clinical psychologists, we also work with individuals who have experienced sexual abuse—we know the extent to which these experiences negatively affect people throughout their lives. As professors who conduct research in sexual violence prevention, we know what the data says about sexual offending behavior, and we know that much of what the general public believes about sexual offenders is not accurate. That is not to suggest that the danger is not real—it is—but the truth may be different than what many believe. Having accurate knowledge is one of the best and most fundamental ways to protect your children.

The Centers for Disease Control and Prevention estimates that one in six boys and one in four girls are sexually abused before the age of eighteen.[1] That is a frightening statistic—but it is a real one and one that we cannot and should not avoid out of anxiety or fear. Whether comfortable or not, we want to help transform fear-based avoidance into proactive information-gathering and knowledge.

In writing this book, we hope to empower you as parents with the knowledge to keep your children safe. The fact that you are being proactive and reading this book puts you one step ahead of the game. You will learn in Chapter 1 that there are many misconceptions about sex offenders. In response to that, we provide you with accurate, research-based information to ensure that your efforts in keeping your children safe are properly targeted. For example: you would not give your child a Band-Aid to treat a fever; in the same way, when you are educating yourself, your child, and your community, you must take similar care to gather the proper information before you make a decision. If you do not have the correct information, you cannot make the correct decisions.

While we wish there was something we could do as parents to keep our children 100 percent safe, this, in reality, is not possible. However, what we can do is equip you with research-based data, evidence-based guidance, and concrete steps that you can take to minimize these risks. While there is no surefire way to avoid the unexpected in life, information is power. That power may give us

---

1   Centers for Disease Control and Prevention, "Adverse Childhood Experiences Study: Data and Statistics. Atlanta," GA: Centers for Disease Control and Prevention, National Center for Injury Prevention and Control, 2005. Retrieved from https://www.cdc.gov/violenceprevention/acestudy/index.html

just a little bit of an edge, and as parents we strive to have every little edge we can to keep our children safe from harm.

We will also review risks for your children throughout childhood, adolescence, and young adulthood, as these risks change as your children grow and develop. When children are young, we have much more control over their environment, but as they become older and turn into adolescents, as parents we must adapt and continue to learn about new risks.

Each chapter is arranged similarly: we present an overview of the topic, highlighting key facts in boxes. Each chapter will culminate with a series of takeaway points and strategies you can employ to protect your children. While many of us like to skip around parenting books to the parts that are important or relevant to us, we recommend that you read the book from the beginning. The first few chapters include the most factual information and set the stage for the rest of the book.

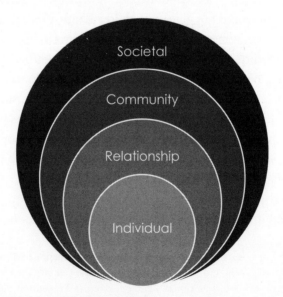

Based upon CDC Social-Ecological Model,
www.cdc.gov/violenceprevention/overview/social-ecologicalmodel.html

There are also a series of discussion group topics at the end of the book. Having open discussions about this material is very important to developing sexual violence prevention strategies in your family, school, and community. While parents can individually decrease the risk for their own children, it is only though larger school, community, and social efforts that a significant dent in the sexual violence problem can be made. As authors of this book, mothers, and researchers, we appreciate you taking this first step to open the dialogue about sexual violence. By bringing this issue out of the dark, we can prevent future harm.

Elizabeth Jeglic, PhD, and Cynthia Calkins, PhD

CHAPTER 1

Myths and Realities: Knowledge Is Power

How would you describe a sex offender? In all likelihood, you would describe a monster—someone who lurks behind bushes and rapes unsuspecting women or abuses children. And that is how sex offenders are portrayed in the media. For most of us, much of what we know about sex offenders comes from movies, TV shows, and news stories. However, those stories are often sensationalized portrayals—or cases that are the exception to the rule—rather than the norm. While cases like these do exist, they remain statistically rare, in that they happen very infrequently. In this chapter, we are going to review the myths and realities of sex offenders and sex offending behavior. While this chapter may make you feel a bit like you are back in school, it is one of the most important chapters in the book as it provides a foundation upon which the other chapters are built. It is important that, as parents, you know the true facts—knowledge is power. We have set up this chapter in a myth versus fact format, as myths about sex offenders abound, and it is important to separate myth from reality.

Myth: Most sex offenses are committed by strangers.
Fact: The large majority of sex offenders are known to the victim.

This is perhaps one of the most dangerous and most important myths about sexual offending. Most people imagine sex offenders as strangers lurking in the bushes or driving white vans. This is categorically untrue. The vast majority of sex offenders are known to their victim. Fewer than 10 percent of children are assaulted by a stranger.

One study[2] found:

- 34 percent of children were assaulted by a family member,
- 59 percent of children were assaulted by an acquaintance, and
- 7 percent of children were assaulted by a stranger.

This knowledge is incredibly important because it shows that many of us are scared of the wrong people. This is what we call the *stranger danger* phenomenon. It is the belief that sex crimes are predominantly committed by strangers when, in reality, they are most often committed by those who are known to us and to our children. What is even scarier is that many of our laws and policies are based on this stranger danger myth. As a consequence of the stranger danger myth, we no longer let our children walk to their friends' houses or the park by themselves—but we readily drop them off for playdates or leave them with family members, babysitters, and community leaders, often without so much as a second thought about their safety and security.

---

2   Snyder, H. N. 2000. *Sexual Assault of Young Children as Reported to Law Enforcement: Victim, Incident, and Offender Characteristics.* Washington, DC: US Department of Justice, 2000.

Myth: All sex offenders will reoffend.

Fact: Only a small percent of released sex offenders will reoffend sexually.

There is a common belief that all sex offenders will reoffend, and thus the majority of our sexual violence prevention policies are based on this assumption. In reality, however, sex offenders have the lowest reoffense rates of all types of offenders. Over a three-year period, the Bureau of Justice Statistics found that only 5 percent of released sex offenders committed another sex crime.[3]

The most comprehensive study to date used a sample of almost 20,000 released sex offenders, and researchers found that over a period of five to six years:

- 13.7 percent of all types of sex offenders reoffended sexually[4] and
- 12.4 percent of all child molesters reoffended sexually.[5]

While these rates are not zero, they are not 100 percent either. Given that there is no psychological profile of a sex offender (see next myth), it is easiest to focus on those who have already committed a sexual offense, since there is an increased likelihood they will do it again if they have done it once before. But as we see from the statistics, most sex offenders will not reoffend sexually.

3   Bureau of Justice Statistics. 2003. *Recidivism of sex offenders released from prison in 1994*. Washington, DC: US Department of Justice, 2003.

4   Hanson, R. K., and K. E. Morton-Bourgon. 2005. The characteristics of persistent sexual offenders: A meta-analysis of recidivism studies. *Journal of Consulting and Clinical Psychology* 73(6): 1154–63.

5   Hanson, R. K., and M. T. Bussiere. 1998. Predicting relapse: A meta-analysis of sexual offender recidivism studies. *Journal of Consulting and Clinical Psychology:* 66: 348–62.

An important study[6] was done in New York State where researchers examined all the new sex crimes that took place over a twenty-year period. They found that only 5 percent of all new sex crimes were committed by someone who had previously committed a sex offense. That means 95 percent of the sex offenders were unknown to authorities before their crime occurred.

This New York study has important implications for sexual violence prevention. Our current sex offender laws and policies focus almost exclusively on already detected sex offenders—the ones who commit 5 percent of the new sex crimes—and very few resources are dedicated to prevent the abuse caused by the other 95 percent. These policies are already very costly, and there is not much money dedicated to prevention. In other words, the lion's share of the resources go to preventing only a small part of the overall offenses. These laws can also give us a false sense of security: by focusing on a tiny sect of the population known to have committed crimes, we ignore less obvious, but in fact much larger, risks. In Chapter 2, you will learn about some of these laws, including sex offender registries.

Myth: There is a specific type of a person who becomes a sex offender.
Fact: There is no sex offender profile, and we still do not know what makes some people commit sexual offenses.
Profiling shows on television make it look like it is easy to figure out who committed a crime because of certain personality and behavioral characteristics (i.e., a profile) associated with criminal offenses. There has been a lot of research done to try and

---

6   Sandler, J. C., N. J. Freeman, and K. M. Socia 2008. Does a watched pot boil? A time-series analysis of New York State's sex offender registration and notification law. *Psychology, Public Policy and Law* 14(4): 284–302. doi:10.1037/a0013881.

determine a sex offender profile, but what the research has in fact shown is that there is no specific profile for those who commit sexual offenses.[7] In general, those who are involved in the criminal justice system tend to be less educated and have lower incomes, but this is not the case for sex offenders, as neither socioeconomic status nor level of education are risk factors for sexual offending behavior. Sex offenders come from all strata of society—they can be unemployed, but they can also be lawyers, doctors, educators, and members of the clergy. Some people assume that those who have been abused themselves are at much higher risk of committing sexual abuse. But the evidence here is thin. One important study showed that only physical abuse and neglect—and not childhood sexual abuse—predicted future sexual offending behavior.[8]

Myth: Sex offenders are "sick."
Fact: The majority of sex offenders do not have a serious mental illness.

One way that we rationalize to ourselves that people could do such heinous acts is to think that there is something wrong with them or that they are sick or mentally ill. While there is some truth to that myth—in that sex offenders do have a higher rate of serious mental illness, including disorders such as schizophrenia and bipolar disorder, than the general population—the large majority of sex offenders are not seriously mentally ill.

One study found that 24 percent of all sex offenders had been hospitalized for a psychiatric problem as compared to 5 percent

7   Marshall, W. L. 1996. The sexual offender: Monster, victim, or everyman? *Sexual Abuse: A Journal of Research and Treatment* 8(4): 317–35.

8   Widom, C. S. and C. Massey. 2015. A prospective examination of whether childhood sexual abuse predicts subsequent sexual offending. *JAMA Pediatrics* 169(1): 1–7.

of the general population.[9] This means that while the rates of mental illness are higher among sex offenders, more than 75 percent of them do not have a serious mental illness. It is thus difficult to understand how and why someone would commit a sex crime—and that is precisely what researchers are trying to figure out.

Myth: Only men commit sexual offenses.
Fact: While it is true that most sex offenses are committed by men, women also commit sex offenses.
Many may find it hard to imagine that women commit sex offenses, but they do. Official sexual abuse data indicates that females perpetrate between 4 to 10 percent of all reported sexual assaults.[10] It has been suggested that the rates of sexual abuse committed by women are in fact higher, but go unreported. We have all watched with interest cases such as that of Mary Kay Letourneau, the Washington State school teacher who was incarcerated for sexually abusing her twelve-year-old student (and who later married that student upon her release from prison), but most female-perpetrated sex crimes take place in the context of caregiving activities. Therefore, it is sometimes more confusing for the child to know whether he or she has been victimized, and even if they feel that anything has happened at all, so much so that they do not report it. One of the reasons female sex offenders go undetected or unreported is due to our social beliefs that men cannot be sexually assaulted by women or that women are nurturers and thus would not hurt a child. While the vast majority of

9 Fazel, S., G. Sjöstedt, N. Långström, and M. Grann. 2007. Severe mental illness and risk of sexual offending in men: A case-control study based on Swedish national registers. *Journal of Clinical Psychology* 68(4): 588–96.

10 Center for Sex Offender Management. March 2007). Female Sex Offenders. http://www.csom.org/pubs/female_sex_offenders_brief.pdf

women do not harm children, there are some that do. Data from the Centers for Disease Control and Prevention (CDC) reported that women perpetrated half of the non-penetration sexual abuse reported by men.[11]

Myth: Only adults commit sex offenses.
Fact: About one-third of all sex crimes against children are committed by someone under the age of eighteen.
This includes what we more traditionally think of as date rape among adolescents, but it also includes young people who offend against children under the age of twelve and whose offense behaviors mirror that of child molesters as opposed to rapists.[12] About one in eight youth who commit sexual offenses are under the age of twelve.

The research shows that youth who commit sexual offenses are different from adults who commit sexual offenses. While most adult sex offenders act alone, about 15 percent of all youth who commit sexual offenses do so in groups. About 12 percent of these offenses take place at school. Further, they are more likely to offend against those known to or related to them. Finally, when youthful offenders target victims under twelve, they are more likely to offend against boys.

Youth who commit sexual offenses are more likely to be male, and only 7 percent of all reported cases are females. However, girls who commit sexual offenses tend to be younger than

11 Black, M. C., K. C. Basile, M. J. Breiding, S. G. Smith, M. L. Walters, M. T. Merrick, J. Chen, and M. R. Stevens. 2011. The National Intimate Partner and Sexual Violence Survey (NISVS): 2010 Summary Report. Atlanta, GA: National Center for Injury Prevention and Control, Centers for Disease Control and Prevention.

12 Finkelhor, D., R. Ormrod, M. Chaffin, M. December 2009. Juveniles who commit sex offenses against minors. *US Department of Justice, Office of Justice Programs*, 1–11. https://www.ncjrs.gov/pdffiles1/ojjdp/227763.pdf

boys—31 percent of girls are under the age of twelve when they commit their offense.

Myth: Youth who commit sexual offense go on to become adult sex offenders.
Fact: The majority of youth who commit sexual offenses do not commit another sexual offense in adulthood.

The good news is that youth who commit sex crimes before the age of eighteen rarely go on to become adult sex offenders. It is estimated that between 7 and 13 percent of those who commit a sexual offense as a minor will commit another offense over a five-year period.[13] The number that will commit another sex offense once they reach adulthood is even less: estimates put it at fewer than 10 percent.

Myth: Most sex crimes take place in public areas like parks.
Fact: Most sex crimes against children take place in private settings.

There has been a lot of debate in parenting forums about "free-range parenting," which entails—in part—letting children hang out in the neighborhood and go to parks unsupervised. While this was normal behavior in our youth, in more recent years cultural norms have changed. Parents have actually been investigated, and sometimes charged with neglect, for leaving their children in parks by themselves. One reason for this strong reaction is the fear that children who are unsupervised in the community will fall prey to a sexual predator. In one of our own studies, we found that only about half of one percent (0.5 percent) of all the sexual offenses in a sample of nearly 1,500 sexual offenses took place in a public location, such as a park or a school, and

---

13 Richards, K. 2011. What makes juvenile offenders different from adult offenders? *Trends & Issues in Crime and Criminal Justice* 409: 1–8.

were perpetrated by a stranger against a child victim. In another one of our studies, we found that 75 percent of individuals who committed a sexual offense met their victims in private (typically residential) settings.[14, 15] This also ties in with the research on who is a sex offender. As we talked about before, we are often worried about our children getting snatched from the street and the playground, but most offenders get to know their victims in more intimate settings because they are family, friends, and community members. Thus, as you will read about in the next chapter, the laws created to keep sex offenders away from areas in which children hang out do little to keep them safer, because this is not where the crimes are occurring.

Myth: Child molesters spontaneously attack when they find a victim.

Fact: Many child molesters engage in what is known as grooming behaviors.

When many of us think about sex offenses, we think about the stranger in the white van or the Central Park rapist who lurks about and grabs their victims. However, these types of crimes are exceptionally rare. In reality, many of those who molest children use "grooming," which refers to the behaviors that the sexual offender engages in before abusing the child. This usually involves gaining the trust of the child and parents so that the abuse can take place without detection. Research suggests that

---

14 Colombino, N., C. C. Mercado, and E. Jeglic. 2009. Situational aspects of sexual offending: Implications for residence restriction laws. *Justice Research and Policy* 11: 27–43. doi:10.3818/JRP.11.2009.27.

15 Calkins, C., N. Colombino, T. Matsuura, and E. Jeglic. 2015. Where do sex crimes occur? How an examination of sex offense location can inform policy and prevention. *International Journal of Comparative and Applied Criminal Justice* 39(2): 99–112.

about half of all cases of child abuse involve grooming.[16] However, it is believed that grooming is actually much more common; it escapes detection because these grooming behaviors often make the child much less likely to report the abuse. Many of the more famous cases you have heard of in the media, such as the sexual abuse within the Catholic Church and Jerry Sandusky, involved grooming tactics used to build connections with the victims and gain the support of the parents to avoid detection.

Myth: Most sex offenders were abused as children.
Fact: The link between childhood abuse and perpetration is far from clear.

Most individuals who are sexually abused in childhood do not perpetrate offenses against others. In fact, only a small minority of them do. While the general public often assumes that childhood trauma and abuse can lead to sexual offending, researchers are not certain about the connection. What's clear is that there are many pathways to committing abuse. Sexual abuse may certainly play a role for some offenders, but it has not been isolated as an important causal factor.[17] In fact, research shows that childhood neglect puts people at greater risk of committing abuse than childhood sexual abuse does.

Myth: Sex offenders are incurable.
Fact: Most sex offenders will not commit another sex offense once they have been identified.

There is a considerable body of research showing that the risk for sex offending decreases across the lifespan, such that as those

---

16 Winters, G. M. and E. L. Jeglic. 2016. Stages of sexual grooming: Recognizing potentially predatory behaviors of child molesters. *Deviant Behavior* 38(6): 1–10. doi: 10.1080/01639625.2016.1197656.

17 Widom, C. S. and C Massey. 2015. A prospective examination of whether childhood sexual abuse predicts subsequent sexual offending. *JAMA Pediatric* 169(1). doi: 10.1001/jamapediatrics.2014.3357.

who have committed sexual offenses get older, the likelihood that they will commit new sex crimes decreases.[18]

This also ties in to the question as to whether sex offenders can be treated. Most known sex offenders will receive some treatment either in prison or once they return to the community. There is a lot of debate about whether sex offender treatment works, and the jury is still out on this question. The most recent meta-analytic study (a big study that combines the findings of all existing studies to date) looking at whether sex offender treatment works found that offenders who attend sexual offender group treatment programs are less likely to reoffend than offenders who are not offered treatment (10.1 percent treated versus 13.7 percent untreated).[19] While this difference may be small, the consequences of sexual abuse are so large that even a small reduction is meaningful.

Will those who have committed sex offenses always have urges to offend? We have yet to answer that question. What we do know, however, is that this may not matter. Research shows that there are quite a few people in our society who have deviant and often illegal sexual thoughts and desires, but who do not act on them. Further still, we know that some sex offenders do not have deviant or illegal thoughts or fantasies, yet they commit sexual crimes nonetheless. Results from studies that look at treatment effectiveness look promising, and it seems better to continue to develop and test our treatment approaches rather than simply assuming that offenders cannot be helped.

---

18 Harris, D. A. and R. M. Cudmore. 2015. Desistance from sexual offending. *Oxford University Press, Handbooks Online.* doi: 10.1093/oxfordhb/9780199935383.013.77

19 Schmucker, M., and F. Lösel. 2015. The effects of sexual offender treatment on recidivism: An international meta-analysis of sound quality evaluations. *Journal of Experimental Criminology* 11(4): 597–630. doi:10.1007/s11292-015-9241-z.

Take Home Message

Now that you have all these facts, what do you do with this knowledge? As mentioned at the beginning of the chapter, knowledge is power. Some of this knowledge may have been new to you, and perhaps your own personal sexual prevention efforts may have been misguided. This information is not meant to scare you—rather, we aim to give you the resources to better target your prevention strategies. Some of this knowledge may make you more afraid (that anyone can be a sex offender); or, it may make you more comfortable letting your children out in the world. For example, knowing that most sex offenders are family and acquaintances may help you to be more vigilant of the people you leave your children with. On the other hand, knowing that few sex offenders are strangers and that sex offenses don't often happen in public spaces, it may be safer than you thought to let your child play outside or in the local park.

Some of this knowledge is overwhelming, and as parents, we get that. Anytime we let children out of our sight, there are dangers, both sexual and otherwise, from the world around them. However, we hope that by knowing the facts, we will all be better equipped to send our children out in the world aware of the risks, but also aware of what can be done to mitigate some of those risks.

Box 1

Key Fact: Only 7 percent of sex offenses against children were perpetrated by a stranger. The rest of the perpetrators were family, friends, or acquaintances of the victim.

Key Fact: It is estimated that about 10 percent of sex offenders are female and that about one third of all sexual abuse against children is committed by someone under the age of eighteen.

Key Fact: Most sex offenders meet and assault their victims in private locations (like homes) and not in public places like parks.

Key Fact: Most sex offenders will not commit another sex crime once they are caught.

Key Fact: About 95 percent of sex offenses are committed by someone who has never been arrested for a sexual offense before.

CHAPTER 2

What Sex Offender Registries Do (and Do Not Do)

Every US state is required by law to have an online searchable database that you can use to find out if any registered sex offenders live in your neighborhood. Many countries other than the United States—such as Canada, the United Kingdom, Australia, and New Zealand—also have sex offender registries, but they may not be publicly available or may be accessible only to law enforcement. Links to these sex offender registries can be found at the end of this chapter. While it might seem like having access to this knowledge would help to keep your children safe, research is less clear about whether registries and notification laws are helpful in preventing sexual violence. In this chapter, we will share a little bit about the history of sex offender registries, describe what they do, and also review the evidence to see whether they work.

I've heard about Megan's Law—what does that have to do with sex offender registration and notification laws?
In 1994, seven-year-old Megan Kanka of Hamilton, New Jersey, went out for a bike ride when she encountered neighbor Jesse Timmendequas, a man who invited Megan into his home with

the promise of seeing a puppy. Instead of showing her the puppy, Timmendequas raped and killed Megan, dumping her body in a nearby park. That day was a nightmare made into reality for Megan's parents, who would never see their daughter alive again. Adding insult to injury was what came next, information that might have spared Megan her life. Timmendequas, the man living across the street from Megan's family, was a twice-convicted sex offender who had recently been released from prison.

How did Megan Kanka's death lead to widespread proliferation of notification laws in the US?

If a crime like this could happen in a quiet little town like Hamilton, New Jersey, many felt it could happen anywhere else. The details of the crime shook the residents of New Jersey, and later the nation, with fear and horror resonating far beyond the township of Hamilton. As it turned out, not only did Timmendequas have a history of sex crimes, but his two roommates also had a checkered past—in fact, he had met both roommates while in a prison treatment facility for those convicted of sexual crimes.

Public outcry following the Kanka case led parents to want to know who was living in their neighborhoods and communities. Timmendequas, for example, lived thirty yards from the Kanka family, and yet they had no idea he was a sex offender. After the tragic event, Megan's parents and community members began to entertain the thought that we should indeed know about those who pose a risk to us. Within months of her murder, "Megan's Law" was enacted in New Jersey. This law would make information about individuals convicted of sex crimes available to the public. Although too late for Megan's family, it was believed that this kind of information could help prevent the occurrence of future sex crimes. Within two years of Megan's death, the US federal government passed the Wetterling Act, requiring states to notify the public of the addresses of convicted sexual offenders.

So all states are now required to have community notification laws?

Yes. And now federal law makes these notification requirements even tougher for sex offenders. In 2006, the Sex Offender Registration and Notification Act (SORNA) was signed into law by then-President George W. Bush[20]. SORNA was part of the Adam Walsh Child Protection and Safety Act, named for Adam Walsh, a young boy who was abducted from a shopping mall and murdered. His father, John Walsh (host of *America's Most Wanted*), was a strong advocate to get the bill signed into law so he could prevent what had happened to his son from happening to other children. As a result, all states have to comply with SORNA's federal standards. SORNA also made the rules even stricter for sex offenders. Offenders are required to register for longer periods of time, sometimes for life. SORNA also expanded the scope of registration laws, such that juveniles age fourteen years and older who have committed sexual offenses are also required to be on the sex offender registry.

In the United States, SORNA requires that each state maintain an Internet-based registry of all convicted sex offenders. This registry must have information such as the individual's photograph, home address, work address, physical description, and details about the crime he or she committed. Some states add additional information, such as license plate numbers, vehicle descriptions, or the option to track the offender.

Other countries have versions of this type of registration and/or notification schemes. In the United Kingdom, there is the Child Sex Offender Disclosure Scheme (also known as "Sarah's Law") where parents, guardians, and caregivers can formally ask the police to tell them if someone has been convicted of a child sexual offense; Kenya has enacted a similar policy. South Korea, like the

---

20   Adam Walsh Child Protection and Safety Act of 2006. 42 USC § 16901.

United States, has a public sex offender registry containing twelve points of information about convicted sex offenders, including name, address, employment, photograph, physical description, and vehicular registration number. In Canada, Australia, and Taiwan, a registry with information similar to that of the United States has been created, but it is only available to the police and not publicly available. Similarly, in New Zealand a sex offender register has been created, but it is not publicly accessible and is used more as a community supervision strategy so that police and caseworkers can see if there are changing circumstances with the individual.

Do sex offender notification laws make sense?

Few would doubt the sensibility of laws that notify us of dangerous offenders living in our vicinity. After all, doesn't it make sense that our communities would be safer if we knew where all the convicted sex offenders were living? Well, as it turns out, not really. What seems on the surface to be a very simple and good idea does not actually work so well. In fact, there is no data showing that these laws have had any real effect on the overall incidence of sexual violence, whether on a local or national scale. How could this be? As discussed in the previous chapter, these laws are based around the stranger danger myth of offending, and as a result, their impact has been limited. Most offenses are committed by people already known to the victim. Not the neighbor down the block whose image you are seeing for the first time when you click the photo on your state's registry website, but rather the person you invite over to your house or the person already living in your house who is comfortably watching the TV while you read this. No one likes to think that the individuals we know and love—fathers, mothers, brothers, boyfriends, uncles, neighbors, babysitters, coaches, and friends—will harm us. But data reveal that acquaintances and family members are overwhelmingly the perpetrators of sex crimes.

Does this mean that you shouldn't use the registry to look up who lives in your neighborhood? No, it doesn't. We recommend that parents look on the state's registry if they are so inclined. If you are considering hiring a new babysitter, bringing a new boyfriend into the home, or allowing your children to sleep over at someone else's house, it might not be a bad idea to check the registry.

Do sex offender notifications laws work?

Not really. Due to the reasons outlined above, these laws have unfortunately done little to lower rates of sexual violence. A study sponsored by the US Department of Justice analyzed the sexual offense rates in New Jersey ten years before and ten years after the implementation of notification laws[21]. Although the sex offense rates decreased during the span of the study, the most significant decline actually occurred before Megan's Law was passed. In another study, one that examined registration and notification laws in fifteen US states, it was found that notification laws do impact the rate of sexual offenses. However, this impact was not as expected, as notification laws seemed to encourage, rather than discourage, recidivism[22]. These studies, which have been done in different states and countries and across different time periods, generally agree on one thing: that sex offender notification laws have had little, if any, impact on rates of violence.

But how can this be? Wouldn't knowing the names and locations of the bad guys out there protect us? Not a whole lot, it turns out. As we highlighted in Chapter 1 of this book, the many

---

21 Zgoba, K. M. and K. Bachar. April 2009. Sex offender registration and notification: Limited effects in New Jersey. *National Institute of Justice, Office of Justice Programs.*

22 Prescott, J. J., and J. E. Rockoff. 2011. Do sex offender registration and notification laws affect criminal behavior? *Journal of Law and Economics* 54(1): 161–206.

myths and misconceptions about sex offenders have formed the basis for many of our laws today. Most offenders do not commit offenses against stranger victims. The majority of sex crimes— some 75 to 93 percent—are committed by someone known to the victim[23],[24]. Rates of sexual reoffending among known offenders are also somewhat lower than is commonly assumed. Whenever we talk to people about our work with sex offenders, they often express the sentiment that "they all reoffend." However, as you learned in the first chapter, the majority of known offenders will not go on to commit a new sexual offense. Additionally, most new offenses (95 percent) are committed by someone *not* on a sex offender registry[25].

So should I use sex offender registries?

This is a hard question to answer. As we mentioned, the research shows that sex offender notification laws do not prevent sexual violence. However, the main point of this book, again, is that knowledge is power. You want to make sure that the people supervising your children do not have a history of sexual offending. While we know that most sex offenders do not reoffend, you do not want to tempt fate by leaving your child unattended with someone who has a history of sexual violence. We have both accessed the registry to see who in our communities has

---

23 Planty, M., L. Langton, C. Krebs, M. Berzofsky, and H. Smiley-McDonald. 2016. *Female victims of sexual violence, 1994–2010*. Washington, DC: Bureau of Justice Statistics, 2016.

24 Colombino, N., C. C. Mercado, and E. L. Jeglic. 2009. Situational aspects of sexual offending: Implications for residence restriction laws. *Justice Research and Policy* 11: 27–43.

25 Sandler, J. C., N. J. Freeman, and K. M. Socia. 2008. Does a watched pot boil? A time-series analysis of New York State's sex offender registration and notification law. *Psychology, Public Policy and Law 14(4): 284–302.* doi:10.1037/a0013881.

committed a sexual offense. The main purpose for doing so was to ensure that no one whom our children are in contact with (such as neighbors, store owners, friends' parents, etc.) has a history of sexual violence. As researchers and forensic clinicians, we have learned that the best predictor of future behavior is past behavior.

That said, just because someone is not on the registry doesn't mean they are not capable of offending. Many sex crimes go unreported, and thus people may have histories we don't know about. Again, as noted above, a large majority of all new sex crimes are committed by someone *not* listed on the registry.

Are there other types of sex offender laws besides sex offender registries?

The increasing public fear about sex crimes and a desire to do something—anything—to prevent crimes like the assault and murder of Megan Kanka has led to the creation of a lot of laws targeting those who have committed sexual offenses. Another type of controversial law here in the United States is residence restrictions. These statutes, which are created on a local or state level, prevent those convicted of sexual offenses from living and sometimes loitering (hanging out) or working between 500 to 2,500 feet of what is considered a child-dense area, such as school, parks, day care centers, and bus stops.

These residence restriction laws make a lot of sense on the surface: they keep dangerous sex offenders away from places where groups of children come together to learn, play, or otherwise gather. However, once again, these laws are based on the concept of stranger danger, which assumes that sex offenses against children are committed by strangers; in reality, up to 93 percent of cases are committed by someone known to the child[26]. Less than half of one percent of all sex crimes against minors are committed by offenders who are strangers against children in public settings. These laws are thus designed to combat a type of sexual offense that is extremely uncommon. What we have learned through research is that these laws also have unintended consequences. Sex offender registries and residence restrictions make it exceptionally hard for offenders to find a place to live, find employment, and reintegrate into their communities.[27, 28] And in some jurisdictions, it is not just difficult to find a job or housing, but impossible, leaving offenders homeless or transient.

But is it such a bad thing to make life hard for those who have committed sexual offenses?

Yes. By preventing those who have committed sexual offenses from finding employment, obtaining affordable housing, facilitating prosocial connections, and maintaining ties to the community, laws such as these may inadvertently *increase* the risk that offenders pose, as observed in the multistate study cited earlier. A good example of this phenomenon is shown in the movie *The Woodsman*, starring Kevin Bacon. Despite serving his time for a sex offense, once released he is shunned and harassed by the community, attacked at his job, and has little hope that his life will improve. This causes him stress and depression, leading him

---

26 Snyder, H. N. 2000. *Sexual Assault of Young Children as Reported to Law Enforcement: Victim, Incident, and Offender Characteristics.* Washington, DC: US Department of Justice, 2000.

27 Levenson, J. S., D. A. D'Amora, and A. L. Hern. 2007. Megan's law and its impact on community re-entry for sex offenders. *Behavioral Sciences & the Law* 25(4): 587–603.

28 Levenson, J. S. and L. P. Cotter. 2005. The effect of Megan's Law on sex offender reintegration. *Journal of Contemporary Criminal Justice* 21(1): 49–66.

to think, "What's the point of not offending again if life on the outside is like this?"

A few years back, at an academic conference devoted to the assessment and treatment of sexual abusers, treatment providers, parole officers, and professors like ourselves spent the day in colorless hotel conference rooms, listening to the results of carefully conducted studies. One session in particular stood out to us. The presenter was Patty Wetterling, the mother of Jacob Wetterling. Jacob was eleven years old when he was abducted, sexually violated, and left for dead. Like Megan Kanka, Jacob had been out riding his bike that day in St. Joseph, Minnesota. At the time of Jacob's abduction, his parents were surprised to learn that authorities did not have a list of registered sex offenders to consult for potential suspects. Patty eventually stood before Congress encouraging the enactment of a national registry of offenders: a place to start the search should an unthinkable crime like this happen. Indeed, the intent behind these original registration laws was to provide a means for authorities to track and locate individuals convicted of sexual crimes. Registration laws would later evolve to include notification laws—popularized by the case of Megan Kanka—which added to the registry an additional component of community notification.

At the conference, Patty Wetterling spoke about her son Jacob and his love of riding bikes and guacamole, but she also highlighted how that legislation had evolved into something much bigger and, surprisingly, more troubling than she originally envisioned. The registration laws she had lobbied to enact required only that authorities had a list of offenders; today, however, notification laws go much further, making that list public and easily searchable, and requiring offenders, including children as young as nine years old in some states, to be on public websites for decades, sometimes even a lifetime. Patty—an unlikely opponent of this type of legislation—made a powerful argument that day at the conference that notification laws may have gone too far. By making life so difficult for registered sex offenders—especially youthful offenders who end up on the registry as children themselves—we may inadvertently be doing more harm than good in our sexual violence prevention efforts.

Another important reason we should be concerned about these laws is because they cost a lot of money—millions of dollars—to implement and manage. Our tax money is being spent on laws that have been demonstrated to be ineffective at reducing sex crime. What if this money could be better used in a way that actually did lower rates of sexual crime? For example, what if instead of trying to prevent known offenders from committing another sexual crime we were to try to prevent these crimes from happening in the first place?

Take Home Message:
It is *not* our suggestion that concerned parents don't look at sex offender registries to find out who is living in your neighborhood. Rather, we want to inform parents of the limits of this data. Except in rare circumstances, the registry is unlikely to prevent crimes. We hope to bring awareness to the general ineffectiveness of laws such as community notification or residence restrictions so that we, as a community, can begin to redirect our limited resources to legislation that *would* be more likely to make a difference, perhaps even directing our efforts at preventing sexual abuse from happening in the first place.

Box 2

In their 2013 report "Raised on the Registry," the Human Rights Watch detailed the harm of placing children on public sex offender registries in the US. This 111-page report gave voice to the psychological harm, social ostracization, harassment, and even physical violence that those on the registries—often still children themselves—experience. The Human Rights Watch report asks us to consider what these laws hope to accomplish when applied to youth. As detailed in this chapter, it's questionable whether notification laws have had any impact on rates of sexual crime, and there is at least some evidence that notification laws may increase, rather than decrease, rates of sex crime. So should youth, still very much in a period of cognitive and emotional development, be placed on these registries when there is little evidence that these registries work and considerable evidence that they cause harm to youth placed there? Most scientists think that youth should not be placed on the registries, and we—as scientists and mothers—agree.

To access the whole report, check out: www.hrw.org/report/2013/05/01/raised-registry/irreparable-harm-placing-children-sex-offender-registries-us

Box 3: Registry Links

In the US: www.nsopw.gov/

In the UK: www.gov.uk/guidance/find-out-if-a-person-has-a-record-for-child-sexual-offences

In Canada: www.rcmp-grc.gc.ca/to-ot/cpcmec-ccpede/bs-sc/nsor-rnds/index-eng.htm

In New Zealand: www.rcmp-grc.gc.ca/to-ot/cpcmec-ccpede/bs-sc/nsor-rnds/index-eng.htm

In Australia: www.acic.gov.au/our-services/child-protection/national-child-offender-system

CHAPTER 3

How to Start the Conversation

You probably recognize the importance of talking to your children, friends, family, and community about sexual violence prevention. Sexual violence prevention doesn't start with discussions of rape and child molestation; with little kids it is much more basic—discussion of body parts and healthy sexual behavior (at age appropriate levels, of course!). However, you probably also remember those awkward conversations you had during childhood or adolescence when your parents talked to you about sex; or how, in health class, the teacher showed you anatomical diagrams of a male and female genitalia and all the kids started snickering. In our culture, sex is an uncomfortable topic. However, this makes it all the more important to start talking about it early and frequently. This is not confined to a single talk, and it's not just about the mechanics of sex. Rather, it is an ongoing conversation that includes discussion of our bodies, dialogue about concepts such as consent, modeling of healthy relationships, and making oneself available to answer questions and discuss any topic that your child may have questions about. As we will show you over the next several chapters, research in the field and the advice of sex abuse prevention experts is clear: you need to talk to your child about sex, sexual violence, and sexual behavior.

Why do we even have to talk about sex?

Talking about sexuality in an open and honest way is the best method to keep your children safe throughout their lives. The more your children receive the message that talking about their body parts and sexual behavior in general is not shameful, the more likely they are to share information about their bodies with you. Not talking about sex is not a neutral stance. Rather, it sends a clear message to your children that you are not open to communication on this matter. This is what we want: to keep the channels of communication open. For instance, you want your young child to tell you if an adult is touching them in a way that makes them feel uncomfortable, and you want your adolescent to talk to you about what is happening online or at parties so you know where the dangers are and when you may need to step in to help them. Children also model their behavior and attitudes upon those of their parents. If we convey to them that talking about these issues is okay and encouraged, they will do so without shame. However, if we convey to them that there is something shameful about their bodies, they will internalize that, and it will impact their willingness to disclose information.

I don't feel comfortable talking about sex myself—how can I talk to my child about it?

Despite the fact that we are constantly bombarded with sexual images on television and in print, human sexuality is still a topic that makes many of us uncomfortable. It could be the remnants of our own upbringings when we got "the talk," as many of us listened uncomfortably while our parents stumbled awkwardly through the birds and the bees. A recent study found that 19 percent of parents still report feeling uncomfortable talking to their children about sex and about half of teenagers report discomfort talking to their parents about the topic.[29] While most parents reported that they had had multiple conversations with their teens about sex, the majority of the teens indicated that it happened only once or twice. These statistics make it clear that there is a disconnect between what we think we are telling our kids and what they are hearing. Thus, even though it appears that we as a society may be talking about sexuality more openly with our children, it still isn't a regular topic of conversation in most households. Or perhaps it is a regular conversation but just one that's not being heard or internalized by children.

Most of what we know about parent-child communication regarding sex is mainly concerned with adolescent sexual behavior. At present, we still know very little about what is being said to younger children. Most of us have probably heard about "good touch, bad touch" or other such prevention efforts in schools—which will be reviewed in the following chapter—but what, if anything, have you already said to your children about their bodies and sexuality in general? If you are like most people, it feels out of place to use the words *penis* or *vagina* with your toddler or preschooler—but that is exactly what we encourage you to do. Getting into the practice of discussing things openly and directly is a good habit that will help you as your children grow older. Young children spend a lot of time in the bathroom. They poke, they stare, they ask questions. Use this as an opportunity to begin using correct anatomical terms and providing information, and avoid the habit of shutting down their conversations (e.g., "You don't need to know that yet."). While

---

29 Planned Parenthood Federation of America. October 2, 2012. Half of All Teens Feel Uncomfortable Talking to Their Parents about Sex While Only 19 Percent of Parents Feel the Same, New Survey Shows. Retrieved from https://www.plannedparenthood.org/about-us/newsroom/press-releases/half-all-teens-feel-uncomfortable-talking-their-parents-about-sex-while-only-19-percent-parents.

there has been a movement to teach good touch, bad touch (and other prevention programming) in schools, many schools still send home permission forms for parents to sign in order that their children can participate. While the rationale behind this is understandable, it sends the message to parents that this is a taboo topic that requires special permission to discuss. Whether in the bathroom, at home, or at school, we want to remove some of the stigma and shame around these topics so that children can gain knowledge, bring their concerns to trusted adults, and develop a healthy sense of sexuality.

So how do you get over the awkwardness of these discussions? As psychologists, one of the techniques we practice with our clients who have fears is exposure. According to psychological theory, once a fear develops, we tend to avoid it, thus making the fear bigger than it actually is. Therefore, the way to overcome your fears is to tackle them head on and expose yourself to them. For example, most of us were probably not particularly fond of touching feces and vomit before having children; however, now that we are often elbow deep in it, it becomes almost humorous and doesn't cause the same degree of negative reactions anymore. It is really the same as any fear or phobia—like public speaking or fear of spiders—in that the only way to get over it is simply to do it and expose yourself to the feared situation or object. With repeated exposure, the fear eventually lessens. The same can be said for talking about these topics. It may seem strange to call a toddler's sexual organ her vagina, but the more you say it, the more normal it will become to the point where it is second nature, and you will not even remember that it once made you uncomfortable. In the overview to this book, we talked about how avoiding unpleasant things can make them worse; the same goes for talking about sex. So our advice to you is: just do it! It may be hard at first, but it will get easier.

How can I make myself feel better about talking to my children about sexual abuse prevention?

First, it is normal to feel a little uncomfortable talking about sexual abuse with your children. We want to shield our children from pain and hurt, and even thinking that there is a possibility that our children can be abused is very scary for parents. Furthermore, as parents we want to maintain their innocence for as long as we can—to shield them from the big scary world out there. Thus, the first step in starting this process is to do a little work on yourself and your attitudes and beliefs. If our kids sense from us that this in an uncomfortable topic, they, too, will feel uncomfortable talking about it. The earlier you start, the easier and more normal these conversations will be, and the more you will put in place building blocks for a sexual prevention strategy in your own family. For example, when your children are taking a bath, you can review parts of the body: "Show me how you wash your face, show me how you wash your belly, show me how you wash your penis/vagina, etc. . . ." This gives the child the message that these are body parts and that it is okay to talk about them. You also want to be open when children ask you questions about your body or how babies are made. You can give them accurate descriptions that are age appropriate. For example, when children ask about breasts, you can say that women have breasts and that they are used to give babies milk when they are little.

Children are sponges: they pick up our habits—good and bad. If they sense that there is something taboo or shameful about their body parts, they will internalize this. Therefore, to change our own attitudes and beliefs, we use what is called *cognitive restructuring* in psychology, a technique wherein we provide evidence to counter our erroneous beliefs. For example, we sometimes interpret our emotions as facts. If we feel afraid about something, then we tell ourselves that this is something scary that should be avoided. You can also think about it as your brain having two parts—the emotional brain and the logical brain. While we need a good balance of both, when our emotional brain takes over, facts sometimes go out the window. In essence, cognitive restructuring is like arguing with yourself. Your logical self is providing evidence to your emotional self to change your thoughts. This is where the *knowledge is power* theme of the book comes in. We are going to provide you with the knowledge and information you need to challenge your faulty beliefs and thus become more comfortable addressing these issues with your children, your family, and the community.

For example, if you have the belief "talking to my children about sex will damage their innocence" and you therefore avoid having the conversation, you then counter it with fact: "there is no evidence that talking to children and using correct terminology for body parts ruins their innocence; in fact it may even prevent them from being abused, which would truly ruin their innocence" (as you will learn below). The more you are able to do this with yourself, the easier and more natural it will become. Just like riding a bike, changing your way of thinking is a skill—the more you practice, the more natural it becomes. Using these techniques together with the "just do it" approach can help you overcome any trepidation you may have.

Why should I use the correct anatomical names for body parts? Will it ruin my child's innocence?

Sexual prevention educators agree that parents should use the correct anatomical names for body parts. A penis or a vagina is a body part like any other body part. It would never cross your mind *not* to label a head a head or an arm an arm, so why would we think that by calling the penis and vagina by their correct anatomical names we will be hurting our child's innocence? It is the adults that attach sexual meaning to these words; to children they are merely parts of the body like any other part.

Teaching children the correct names for body parts can possibly help prevent child abuse from happening in the first place. In one study, researchers interviewed ninety-one sex offenders who were convicted of molesting children. They asked them various questions about their crime, including how they selected the victims.[30] Some reported that they were less likely to target children who knew the correct anatomical names for body parts as they thought this may increase the risk of them getting caught. There was an assumption— probably a correct one—that because these children were educated about appropriate sexual behavior and safety, they would be more likely to disclose to an adult. These important findings show us that by teaching children the correct names for body parts, we are *not* ruining their innocence; rather we may be protecting it!

What's the harm in using "cutesy" words to describe the genitals?

It may seem harmless enough to use cutesy words to describe the penis and vagina—calling the penis a *peepee*, *weiner*, *dinky*, or *winky*; and the vagina a *hoohoo*, *cookie*, *tee-tee*, or *downstairs*. However, this gives children the message that there is something different or strange about those body parts. Using incorrect terminology can also hamper reporting efforts. One sexual prevention educator recounted the story of how a little girl told her teacher that another child was grabbing her "cookie" (meaning her vagina), and the teacher, thinking that the child was referring to the tasty treat, told the child that it was important to share. This would be a hard misunderstanding to correct since the child did not even know the correct anatomical term.

This also becomes a concern should abuse be reported to authorities—communication may be hampered or impeded and

---

30 Elliot, M., K. Browne, and J. Kilcoyne. 1995. Child sexual abuse prevention: What offenders tell us. *Child Abuse and Neglect* 19(5): 579–94.

could cast reasonable doubt as to what happened to the child, leading to mistrial or prolonged courtroom proceedings.[31] One of the big issues in prosecuting child molesters is that it often becomes a case of the child's word versus that of the child molester. Thus, the more accurately and objectively a child can describe what happened, the more likely he or she is to be believed.

Talking to your children about their body parts will make them engage in sexual behavior earlier.

There is *no* evidence that giving your children the proper anatomical names for their body parts will encourage early sexual behavior. In fact, the opposite is likely true. Teaching children that there is no shame in their body parts is related to better body confidence, which in turn causes higher self-esteem. Research shows that tweens and teenagers who have high levels of self-esteem are three times less likely to engage in early sexual behavior and are half as likely to have a teenage pregnancy.[32, 33]

Sex is a taboo topic in my culture.

While talking about sex may be taboo in many cultures or subcultures, sexual abuse occurs all over the world across all racial, ethnic, and cultural groups.[34] No one is immune. Not talking

---

31 *State v. Watkins*, 318 N.C. 498, 498 (N.C. 1986).

32 Spencer, J. M., G. D. Zimet, M. C. Aalsma, and D. P. Orr. 2002. Self-esteem as a predictor of initiation of coitus in early adolescents. *Pediatrics* 109.4 (2002): 581–84. Print.

33 Dennison, Catherine. 2004. Teenage pregnancy: An overview of the research evidence. Teenage Pregnancy Unit (n.d.): p. 6. Nice.org. 2004. http://www.nice.org.uk/niceMedia/documents/teenpreg_evidence_overview.pdf.

34 Centers for Disease Control and Prevention. June 5, 2015. Prevalence of sexual violence against children and use of social services—Seven countries, 2007–2013. *Morbidity and Mortality Weekly Report* 64(21): 565–69.

about sexual abuse will not make the problem go away. Instead, it keeps it hidden, enabling the offenders to continue hurting children without repercussions. As noted above, talking about body parts does not correlate with sexual behavior and in fact promotes abstention, as comfort with your body can translate to body confidence and self-esteem.

We know it is hard to do things that go against your beliefs or the belief of your community; however, all cultures value children's health and safety, and the long-term repercussions of sexual abuse are well-documented. Furthermore, you are reading this book because you want to keep your children safe. Cultural norms, while often ingrained, do change over time. Given the research and advice of experts, the path to safety is clear—and communication is integral. So while it may be hard, we implore you to start this conversation within your community using the information you learn in this book. One by one, we can all begin to make a difference in changing community norms just by using correct language and talking more openly about these topics.

My kids are already in school, and I haven't started using correct anatomical terms yet—is it too late?

It is never too late. While it may take a word or two of explanation on your part as to why the words for these body parts are changing, children are generally okay with change and accept it more easily than we do as adults. For example, one day, when your children are in the bath, you could say, "When you were little we called your private parts [insert word], but now you are a big kid, and it is important to know that the correct word for this body part is [penis/vagina]. It may be hard to remember at first, but that's okay—I can remind you." As long as you do it in a matter of fact way, it should not be a big deal. If your child asks questions, answer them honestly.

My in-laws refuse to use correct anatomical terms and think we are crazy for talking to our children about this stuff at such a young age. What do I do?

That is fine—not everyone has to be on board with this strategy as long as you are. Your relatives may come from a different generation where there were different rules about how sexual behavior was discussed (or rather not discussed). You probably will not change their minds, though you can certainly share this book with them and the rationale behind your decision to use proper terms. Remember, however, that you are the one who is educating your child, and you spend the most time with them, so the words that your children hear from you are the most important. By the time they hit school age, they will be well aware that there are different words for body parts (particularly those involved in bathroom activities). As long as they know the correct terminology, joking around and using other silly terminology is normal and acceptable childhood behavior.

Take Home Message:

Open lines of communication are important in the prevention and detection of sexual violence. In this chapter, we reviewed why it is so important to talk to your children about sex and why it is vital to start the conversation early. These early decisions you make about how to name your children's body parts and the way in which you talk about subjects related to anatomy, sexual behavior, and sexual abuse prevention set the tone for your communications, as they go through adolescence and early adulthood. In essence, these early steps lay the foundation and set you up to build a strong and open relationship with your children with respect to their willingness to talk to you about traditionally taboo subjects. Using correct anatomical language can in fact prevent your children from being abused, as they are viewed by potential child molesters as savvier and more likely to be educated in sexual violence prevention. Furthermore, open discussion of body parts prevents feelings of shame, which can lead to low self-esteem and engagement in riskier sexual behavior as children transition in adolescence and young adulthood. The words *penis* and *vagina* should become words that are as commonplace and neutral in your household as the words *leg* and *arm*. Remember—building your own comfort level around the topic of sex could one day help to prevent your child from becoming a victim.

Box 4

Sample Dialogue: Young child

When your child is naked—either while getting dressed/undressed or in the bath—is a great time to have such talks.

Parent: *"This is your penis/vagina—this is where you go pee pee* (or the language you use to describe urination)."

Parent: *"Boys and girls have different parts. Your parts look like mommy's/daddy's."*

You will continue this conversation as they grow up, using the correct anatomical names, and it will become second nature to them.

Sample Dialogue: Child three to four years and up

With young children, the topic of genitals will inevitably come up. This is a great time to have the conversation below. If your child doesn't bring it up and is of preschool age, you can bring it up in a casual way when your child is changing or in the bath.

Parent: *"It's important that you know that your penis/vagina is private. No one should be touching your penis/vagina—except the doctor when mommy and daddy are in the room."*

Parent: *"If someone tries to touch your penis/vagina or asks you to touch theirs, it is important to say "no," run away, and tell an adult or mommy/daddy and know that mommy and daddy will never be upset with you."*

If your child has questions, make sure to answer them honestly, but in a reassuring way. For example, if they ask why people would do that, you can say: *"Sometimes people make bad decisions and do things they are not supposed to—so just leave the situation and let an adult know if that happens."* However, it is most likely they will just say okay and continue on with whatever they are doing.

CHAPTER 4

Sexual Abuse Prevention in Schools and Our Community

One of our goals is to help bring the topic of sexual abuse out of the shadows. As noted at the beginning of this book, it wasn't that long ago that sexual abuse was a topic seldom talked about. Little research was devoted to the topic, and barely any of the laws that we have today that pertain to sexual abuse existed. Furthermore, school and community organizations didn't see the topic of abuse as relevant to their curriculum. That is fortunately changing, and the fact that you are reading this book is sign of the times, a new era where parents no longer want to pretend that these problems don't exist. Given all of the media attention dedicated to sexual crimes these days, many readers would probably be surprised to learn that sexual violence has actually *decreased* by up to 50 percent in the last couple of decades.[35] Schools and community organizations began to accept their role as beyond simply the education of children and now are also charged with the protection of children. Due to their regular contact with

---

35 Planty, M., L. Langton, C. Krebs, M. Berzofsky, and H. Smiley-McDonald. 2016. *Female victims of sexual violence, 1994–2010*. Washington, DC: Bureau of Justice Statistics, 2016.

children, school staff are uniquely positioned to look for signs of abuse and to talk to kids about abuse, and schools have begun to be seen as a place where youth can report what's going on in their home or community.

What Is good touch, bad touch?

Some of you may have heard about *good touch, bad touch*, which—at least historically—was a central concept of many popular school-based sexual abuse prevention programs. Typically administered through the school curriculum, good touch, bad touch programs taught personal body safety to young children. These programs focused on raising children's awareness about abuse, educating kids about the private areas of their bodies, and giving them a voice to say "no" to situations that make them uncomfortable. The emphasis of this program was on distinguishing bad touches—those that make a child feel uncomfortable or are confusing—from good touches—touches that a child consents to and that make them feel safe and secure, thus arming kids with the skills to protect themselves.

Children in these programs were sometimes shown videos of dangerous situations or asked to sign a "Bill of Body Rights" contract, which taught them that their body parts were theirs and that they had a right to decide whether others could touch them or not. With empowerment being a goal, children were encouraged to practice verbalizing the word "no," saying it aloud so that one could be prepared to deploy it if necessary. Whether through video, a Bill of Body Rights, or the word *no*, children were in the driver's seat.

But is it a child's responsibility to stop abuse?

No. For this reason, programs like *good touch, bad touch* began to fall out of favor. From an early age, we instill in our children the mind-set that they should respect and pay attention to adults. But then to tell them that not everyone's intentions will be good and that they should be alert to people who may try to hurt them? This can be scary and confusing to kids. Professionals questioned whether it was right to send children to the front lines in the fight against sexual abuse.

For example, it is not unusual for very young children—those below age eight—to be unable to appreciate the concept of inappropriate touch. Much abuse can be disguised as normal behaviors that parents or guardians engage in. For example, offenders often say that they were just bathing children, applying a cream to their genital area, or otherwise engaging in routine caretaking behaviors. Even professionals can have trouble determining if abuse has occurred, especially when offenders work hard to make their behavior ambiguous, which most do. Abuse can also be confusing for older children and teenagers who may have developed a positive relationship to their abuser, who have experienced a pleasurable physical reaction to the abuse, or who either wanted the sexual relations to occur or didn't say no. Thus, they can feel responsible for the abuse, believing themselves to have had some kind of responsibility for the nature of the relationship or the events that took place.

Your children's school may, or may not, have prevention programming in place. If they do, it likely includes some remnants of this early good touch, bad touch model. Many of these newer programs seek to raise awareness of abuse, while being more careful not to put the responsibility of preventing abuse on the child victim. Programs vary widely in the content they cover, in the teaching techniques they employ, and in their comprehensiveness. Some might be a single half hour session while others may use many hours of programming that is integrated into the school health curriculum. We encourage you to find out what program, if any, your school uses to help children learn about sexual abuse. Our review of the research shows generally positive outcomes for age appropriate programs, including increased knowledge about sexual abuse, increased positive feelings about self, earlier disclosure of abuse, and shorter duration of abuse.[36]

How can we be careful not to victim blame?

You may have heard of the term *victim blaming*, which happens when the victim of the crime is somehow held at least in part responsible for their victimization. This is especially true with sex crimes where we have historically been quick to blame victims. With other crimes, we don't think to ask whether the victim was drinking, what they were wearing, or ask them as to why they went somewhere alone. But with sexual assault, we search for answers in the victim's behavior to explain why the perpetrator did what they did. Children who are sexually abused often feel somehow responsible for their own abuse and many report feelings of guilt and shame. Parents can then inadvertently compound these feelings by saying things like, "I told you that you shouldn't have been at that place." Societal awareness has, fortunately, begun to grow around this issue. The responsibility should be on us—and not on our children—to prevent abuse. This growing awareness has begun to change our approach to women, as well. Gone are the legions of bodily defense classes and with it some of the victim-blaming attitudes that have long plagued our society. And with these changing attitudes, victims of assault, whether children or adults, will be less likely to internalize blame and more likely to report assaults or disclose abuse.

So what else can schools and communities do?

Newer, evidence-based approaches to child sexual abuse prevention in schools include a variety of techniques and teaching aims.

---

36 National Sexual Violence Resource Center. 2011. Child sexual abuse prevention: Programs for children.

Among them are activities aimed at building children's confidence and self-esteem. Creating an environment where children can identify their emotions and trust in their own feelings has positive repercussions far beyond that of preventing abuse. Children with a positive self-concept are happier, better equipped to deal with obstacles in their life, and have more trust in their own instincts if something doesn't feel right. Moreover, self-confidence in a child can serve as a deterrent to offenders, who often target children who they see as weak, troubled, or needy, and who may lack the confidence to talk to adults.

Another aspect of this confidence building is bodily autonomy. Prevention programs teach children to correctly label their body parts and to understand that just because someone is an adult doesn't mean that they have the right to tickle, touch, or force playful or loving contact on you. This is an important lesson for us as adults, too. Often, despite protests of "No!" we instruct our children to give Grandma a kiss or hug a friend. How many of us out there have held a child down and tickled them despite their protests of no? While well-intentioned, this has the effect of teaching children that they do not have control over their bodies (rather, adults have control over their bodies) and that the word "no" is devoid of meaning. We can teach kids both bodily autonomy and the right to respect others in every day moments, whether by encouraging them to ask permission when hugging one of their little friends or stepping in when a well-meaning aunt or uncle tries to force a kiss or hug on them, clarifying that the child doesn't want physical contact right now but that they can ask again later. At first blush, this may seem extreme. After all, it's just a hug or some playful fun. But our actions with children send them important messages. And we want to be sure that these messages are the right ones and not ones that lead them to think that they must accept the touch of others or that they have the right to touch others' bodies without consent.

One of the most important things for children to know is that there are adults in their community who can be trusted and who will believe them. Offenders often use grooming strategies with youth, strategies that help to set the stage for abuse to occur. Instilling a belief that adults are unlikely to believe the victim should they disclose the abuse can be part of this process. For example, one victim we worked with described how his perpetrator had set the stage long before his abuse began, putting into motion the idea that the child was someone who lied about things and could not be trusted. Having groomed the family over a period of months—painting the child as a "bad kid"—the perpetrator then groomed the child in a way that family members would be unlikely to believe the child were he to report the abuse. Everyone came to view this child as someone who could not be trusted. And if you know an adult is unlikely to believe you, the only outcome to reporting is angering the perpetrator. Children should know—regardless of their own behavior and what they may have done wrong—that there are adults in their environment who they can talk to and that they can bring concerns to them without repercussion. Children often think that being abused is some fault of their own, and it is our responsibility to instill confidence, encourage dialogue, and create environments built on trust.

What are some examples of modern day prevention programming?

Modern day sexual abuse prevention programs tend to focus more holistically on raising the self-esteem and self-confidence of children and in making the prevention of abuse the responsibility of the community, not the child. For example, the *Stop it Now!* and *Darkness to Light* programs both center on raising awareness about child sexual abuse and empowering parents and community members to prevent, recognize, and/or report abuse. Among those programs that are aimed at children, the "*Who Do You Tell*"™ program,[37] targeted to children ages six to twelve years, uses stories, songs, videos, and role-playing to promote assertiveness and practice open dialogue with trusted adults.

The Catholic Church, rocked by scandal in 2002 following widespread reports of abuse, instituted *Safe Environment Training*.[38] This program, directed at both youth and adults, seeks not only to teach children to recognize abuse but also to change organizational practices and situational factors that promote an unsafe environment. This work focuses on changing institutional culture and routines. Indeed, large national investigations[39,40] into the Church abuse crisis revealed that the problem was less about a few bad apples (i.e., clergy) in the ranks and more about a poisoned tree (e.g., the institutional structure of the church itself—including reporting structures, isolation of clergy, and seminary training inadequate for the purposes of managing a celibate life) that created a culture in which abuse ran rampant.

37 Tutty, L. 1997. Child sexual abuse prevention programs: Evaluating Who Do You Tell. *Child Abuse and Neglect* 21(9): 869–81. doi:10.1016/S0145-2134(97)00048-3.

38 Desai, K. and D. Lew. 2012. Safe environment training: The effectiveness of the Catholic Church's child sexual abuse prevention programs. Houston, TX: *Children at Risk Institute, 2012.*

39 John Jay College of Criminal Justice. 2004. The nature and scope of sexual abuse of minors by Catholic priests and deacons in the United States: A report presented to the United States Conference of Catholic Bishops by the John Jay College Research Team.

40 Terry, K. J., et al. 2011. The causes and context of sexual abuse of minors by Catholic priests in the United States, 1950–2010: A report presented to the United States Conference of Catholic Bishops by the John Jay College Research Team.

Who is to blame when it comes to abuse, the person or the situation?

The *fundamental attribution error* in psychology refers to a *blame-placing* bias that we all share. When we hear about an unfortunate event occurring (e.g., a car accident), we are quick to blame the *person* (i.e., it's Julie's driving skills). But when it is us at the wheel, we blame the situation. The rain. Construction vehicles blocking our way. Potholes in the road. Brakes that don't work right. When we think about sexual violence, our first reaction is to want to find the bad apples. Yet we seldom think about the situations that foster those bad apples. Increasing evidence reveals that, as found by the Catholic Church studies, certain situations heighten the likelihood with which sexual abuse occurs. Work by Stephen Smallbone in Australia has attempted to "design out" opportunities for abuse in school settings.[41] For example, organizational procedures that establish clear rules about staff and student interactions or provide easily accessible and transparent policies for reporting concerns can minimize the incidence of abuse. Enhancing natural surveillance, with windows on doors and easy lines of sight, can serve as a deterrent.

As a thought experiment, imagine yourself as someone who wants to commit a petty offense, such as parking in a restricted zone while you quickly head into an appointment. Your intention to do this is there, but whether or not you actually park your car will be situationally determined. For example, you will probably look around to see if there is a police presence or to see if other cars are ticketed. You might take notice of how many other people are also parked in this illegal zone. Will you be able to see your car from the office of your appointment? Now consider someone who seeks to perpetrate an act of abuse against a child.

---

41 Smallbone, S. 2015. Child safe schools: Can sexual abuse be 'designed out'? Melbourne: Victorian Registration and Qualifications Authority.

Might their willingness to commit an offense be different if there are windows on office doors in the church or child's school, or if they know that there are clear reporting structures in place for those who suspect or want to report abuse? Perhaps there are clear rules about the sorts of behavior that are not allowed (e.g., driving a child home from school or communicating via social media) or perhaps they simply know that this child is educated about sex and has good communication with their parents. The intention or urge may be the same, but the likelihood of committing abuse in certain situations will be lower. Evidence shows this to be true: while it's easy to say that someone who is determined to abuse a child will find a way, data show that changing situational factors will impact rates of offending.

Society's approach to prevention programming has evolved. Early efforts put the onus of the work on the child, but more recent efforts draw attention to our responsibility as adults, as organizations, and as a society to stop abuse. Research findings reveal that situations have a lot more to do with the likelihood that abuse occurs than we think. Some centers are developing innovative prevention programming that give those who struggle with deviant or pedophilic urges, but who have not yet acted on those urges, a place to turn.

Who is required to report abuse?

Mandatory reporting laws came into existence during the 1960s, due in large part to C. Henry Kempe's 1962 publication "The Battered-Child Syndrome"[42], one of the first research studies to bring serious attention to the problem of child sexual abuse. Henry Kempe's publication stirred public discourse and concern, and it brought with it legislative action aimed at preventing or

---

42 Henry Kempe, C., et al. July 7, 1962. The battered-child syndrome. *JAMA* 181(1): 17-24. doi:10.1001/jama.1962.03050270019004.

minimizing abuse. Within three years of Henry Kempe's publication, all fifty states had some sort of mandatory reporting law on the books.[43] These laws require teachers, school administrators, and teachers' aides, among others (e.g., hospital personnel, psychologists and psychiatrists, police officers, day care workers, and social workers), to report suspicions of abuse. Mandated reporters *must*, by nature of their profession, convey suspected incidences of abuse to the appropriate authorities (e.g., Child Protective Services) in their state. Data from the US Department of Health and Human Services show that approximately 69 percent of substantiated abuse and neglect cases are brought to attention of authorities by professionals who report abuse.[44]

43 Leonard G. Brown III and Kevin Gallagher, Mandatory Reporting of Abuse: A Historical Perspective on the Evolution of States' Current Mandatory Reporting Laws with a Review of the Laws in the Commonwealth of Pennsylvania, 59 Vill. L. Rev. Tolle Lege 37 (2015). Available at: http://digitalcommons.law.villanova.edu/vlr/vol59/iss6/5

44 US Department of Health and Human Services, Administration on Children, Youth and Families. 2006. *Child maltreatment 2004*. Washington, DC: US Government Printing Office.

Box 5: Teaching consent to young children

A simple and fun game to teach consent to young children can be played as follows: children break into pairs and take turns asking one another if they can touch them in a particular way. For example, Child A might ask Child B if she can hug them. If Child B says "no," Child A then performs the act on him or herself (i.e., she gives herself a hug). Children get to practice saying "yes" and "no,"—in however an emphatic way they choose (e.g., "absolutely!" or "No way Jose!") to different things, while the person initiating the touch practices respecting boundaries. Switching roles and partners allows young children to have some fun and develop an understanding of permission and respecting rights, while also acting out some silly scenarios, such as bear hugging, kissing, tickling, pinching, giving noogies, or rubbing noses with themselves or their consenting partners. After the game is complete, adults can process the game with children, asking what it was like to be able to consent to touch, discussing whether it was hard to maintain the rules, and encouraging children to understand the importance of both asking for and giving consent.

CHAPTER 5

Keeping the Lines of Communication Open

So you have now started talking to your child about their body parts, and you know the facts about sexual abuse. What are the next steps? Unfortunately, the risk for sexual violence is an on-going one that changes as your children get older. When they are young, you worry about their safety anytime they are not with you, but as they grow, there are new and different dangers associated with access to the Internet, increased independence, and sexual violence at parties and in dating situations. In a sense, it is easier when your children are younger as you have more control over whom they see and what they do; but as they get older and gain more independence, the need for open dialogue becomes even more imperative.

How do we have these kinds of conversations?
There is no right or wrong way to keep the lines of communication open. Some families choose to have regular family meetings where such things are discussed; other families feel more comfortable having the conversations informally. You can do what feels most comfortable to you. However, if you start these conversations when your children are young, it will be easier to

continue open dialogue about these subjects as your children get older. The key is making this dialogue a common topic of conversation so that it doesn't elicit discomfort and anxiety. The formal "sit down talk" of yesteryear should be replaced with on-going, regular informal dialogue.

When children are younger, these talks may be more concrete. Discussion of body parts is most easily done, for example, when the child is naked in the bath or when they are getting dressed or undressed. As children grow up, they are capable of more dialogue and tend to talk to their parents in more informal ways. Thus, the Centers for Disease Control and Prevention (CDC) recommends that informal conversations with your teenagers may work best when the opportunity arises.[45] For example, they suggest that face-to-face conversations may be difficult during the teenage years, and situations such as driving in the car may be ideal times to bring up these topics.

Talking about sexual violence prevention also goes hand in hand with talking about sexuality in general. As much as you want to prevent sexual abuse, you also want to discuss healthy sexual behavior. As discussed in Chapter 3, body confidence (not feeling shame about your genitals and sexuality in general) is related to less risky sexual behavior, which in turn decreases the risk for victimization.[46, 47]

Talking about sex with children and teenagers is a sensitive topic. Your family's view of healthy sexual behavior may

---

45 Centers for Disease Control and Prevention. 2015. Positive Parenting Practices. Available at https://www.cdc.gov/healthyyouth/protective/positive-parenting.htm.

46 Gillen, M. M., E. S. Lefkowitz, and C. L. Shearer. 2006. Does body image play a role in risky sexual behavior and attitudes? *Journal of Youth and Adolescence* 35(2): 230–42.

47 Testa, M. and K. H. Dermen. 1999. The differential correlates of sexual coercion and rape. *Journal of Interpersonal Violence* 14(5): 548–61.

be different from someone else's due to religious, cultural, or personal beliefs about what constitutes healthy sexuality. You may be worried about what your children are hearing and who they are hearing it from because others' views may not match your own. However, in this day and age, short of locking up your children in their rooms, there is no way we can shelter them from this type of information. Thus, the best way to keep your children safe is to have them obtain the information from you. Research suggests that teens who are able to talk with their parents about sex are more likely to delay having sex and engage in safe sex practices when they eventually do have sex.[48] Another survey of teens found that teens generally share their parents' values about sexual behavior and that the decision to delay sex would be easier if they could speak openly to their parents about it.[49]

In order to keep the lines of communication open, the CDC recommends the following:[50]

1. Know where your child is getting information and from whom. You want to make sure that the information your child is receiving is factually and medically accurate and that the views expressed mirror the views you are trying to impart upon your child.

---

48 Markham, C. M., D. Lormand, K. M. Gloppen, et al. March 2010. Connectedness as a predictor of sexual and reproductive health outcomes for youth. *The Journal of Adolescent Health* 46 (Suppl 3): S23–41.

49 Albert, B. 2012. *With one voice: America's adults and teens sound off about teen pregnancy*. Washington, DC: The National Campaign to Prevent Teen and Unplanned Pregnancy. Retrieved February 6th, 2017, from http://thenationalcampaign.org/resource/one-voice-2012.

50 Centers for Disease Control and Prevention. November 2014. Talking with your teens about sex: Going beyond the "talk". Available at https://www.cdc.gov/healthyyouth/protective/pdf/talking_teens.pdf.

2. Be relaxed and open when you speak to your child. If they perceive that you are comfortable talking about this topic, they will more likely approach you in the future.

3. Avoid overreacting. It is common for us as parents to overreact when we hear information we do not like or that scares us, but this could also send the message to our children that they have done something bad, which may make them feel shame or decrease the likelihood of them talking to us in the future.

The CDC and various other organizations have developed resources and programs for helping parents communicate with teenagers about sex and other related topics. Website addresses for these resources are found at the end of this chapter.

How often do I talk about this kind of stuff with my young children?

There is no precise number of times that this should be discussed. Research on parent-child communications suggests that these topics should be discussed frequently enough that it is not an uncomfortable or taboo topic. So what does that mean in terms of frequency? While we cannot point to any evidence to suggest a precise number of times per year, ideally there should be some mention or discussion of the topic every few months. As we learned in Chapter 4, much of this discussion is not taking place in schools, and thus it is up to parents to protect and teach their children. Even if children have had the discussion once or twice, they often forget. Making it a regular topic of conversation in your household will make everyone feel more comfortable to share.

What types of things should I discuss with my young children? I do not want to scare them.

This is a good question and one that parents struggle with: How do you talk about the "bad" things in the world without making your child feel like the world is a bad place? This is especially important with young children, as preschoolers have vivid imaginations—this is the time when they become afraid of monsters and the boogeyman. With this in mind, rather than teaching your children to fear, you can send a message of empowerment. The following three messages can be used to communicate to your children that they are in control of their own bodies and that they should always talk to you if they feel uncomfortable.

1. Teach your children that their body belongs to them and that people should respect their boundaries, just as they should respect others' boundaries. If something doesn't feel good, they have a right to move away and/or ask the person to stop. This may include unwanted tickles, hugs, and kisses. As a parent, you will have to model this behavior and respect when your own child tells you to stop. For example, if you are kissing and tickling your child and they yell "Stop!" you should stop immediately and say, "Thank you for telling me to stop. I appreciate how you used your words to tell me that you did not want me doing that anymore." This shows the child that they can have control over what happens to them and that you as an adult respect that.

2. Teach your children that they should not keep secrets from you. Child molesters often have secrets with their victims to prevent them from revealing the abuse to older adults. For example, they may use a curse word and then say to the child, "Oops—don't tell your parents." Now the child has agreed to keep a small secret. The skilled

child molester can then continue to build these small secrets until the abuse starts, at which point the child has already kept so many secrets from their parents that they may not feel that they can tell. This is the old "foot in the door" technique that door-to-door salesmen used to use. If they can get you to agree to small things—like "May I have a minute of your time"—then it is easier to get you to agree to the bigger things, like buying a vacuum. Let your children know that they should not have secrets with other adults and that it is wrong for adults to tell children to keep secrets. You can let them know that mommy or daddy will never be angry if they tell them anything.

3. Make sure your children know that they will never get into trouble for telling you anything. You can let them know that you are there to love and support them and keep them safe. Convey to your children that if something or someone makes them feel uncomfortable, they should always tell you without fear of consequence or punishment.

The earlier you start with this type of conversation, the easier it will become.

How do I bring up these kinds of issues without it being awkward?

Awkwardness is in the eye of the beholder. If you feel like it is an awkward topic, then your verbal and body language will convey this to your children and they, in turn, will feel awkward. If on the other hand you talk about sexual violence prevention in the same way you would talk about pool safety or wearing sunscreen, your children will not think it is a big deal. Sexuality in our culture is an uncomfortable topic because we have made it that way. This was the message we were given as children, and as a consequence, this secrecy about sex allows for victim-ization to go hidden and undetected. If our children are now given the message that discussing body parts and sexual behav-ior is okay, that takes away power from the abusers. As noted in Chapter 3, convicted child molesters reported that they were more likely to stay away from children who knew anatomical names for body parts because this meant that the children were taught sexual violence prevention strategies and would be more likely to report them. This further reinforces the mantra that knowledge is power.

I have three children—should I talk to them together or separately?

In all likelihood, your children will be at three different ages, which would suggest that the information you will want to share and discuss with them would be different (see Box 7 on page 60). With your preschoolers, you will focus on body part names, body empowerment, and open communication. These themes will continue into the grade school years with a larger focus on Internet safety. Teenagers will face additional challenges related to sexual violence at parties and in dating relationships. Thus, it is important that you tailor your conversations to the develop-mental needs of each of your children according to the issues they are facing at their specific age.

That said, in the spirit of open and honest dialogue, if your older child should ask you something specific while the younger children are present, we encourage you to respond with facts. You may later need to explain that material in a more devel-opmentally appropriate way to younger children. For example, if an older child asks how some complex phenomena (say, rain or snow) happen, you would explain in a direct way, even if this were not comprehensible to the younger child, right? You wouldn't avoid the question.

How do I know what is being discussed at school?

You have a right to know what your child is being taught about sexual violence prevention and sexual health in general. Most schools use a standardized curriculum that they should be willing to share with you if you ask. Some schools will send home notices to inform parents that the discussions will be happening, what will be covered, and also how they can continue the conversation at home—others do not. It is important for parents to know what their children are learning because you want to be able to continue the conversation at home. Ideally, the message and language that is used at school should be the same message that is given at home. This further reinforces to the child that everyone is on the same page and that this type of conversation is normal. You can contact your child's teacher, the school administrator, or a parent-teacher organization to help you obtain this information. It is also important for schools to get the message that this is important to parents. While it is sometimes worrisome when topics such as sexuality are taught to your children by other people, we have to trust that with open lines of communication we can speak to our children about what they are learning. If what they are learning is not in accordance with your own personal beliefs, you can discuss where the discrepancies lie and why you believe the things you do.

Some parents choose to not have their children participate in such discussions. One of our students told us that when sexuality was being introduced as part of the grade six curriculum, all but eight children's parents chose for them not to participate. While it is understandable for parents to feel anxious when such topics are taught by others, what message does this send to our children? That this is something we don't participate in; that it is wrong to learn about healthy sexuality. Parents should work together with the schools to develop and plan curriculum for sexual violence prevention—because when children are knowledgeable and aware, everyone wins.

Should I talk to other parents about this?

Absolutely! Other parents are part of your community. The more these issues are discussed and people are made aware of them in your community, the safer your community will become. Once parents are educated about the realities of sexual violence, then you can discuss how you will develop your own sexual violence prevention initiatives within your community. At the end of this book we have included discussion group questions that can be used to form the basis for these conversations. Ideally, parents can partner with the schools so that they are on the same page with regard to the tone and content of these conversations.

My teen barely speaks to me about anything—how can I get them to talk to them about this?

No one ever said that the teenage years were easy. In many instances, it is hard to talk to your teenager about anything—not to mention sexual violence prevention and healthy sexual behavior. Just because your teen doesn't communicate with you much doesn't mean that they do not listen to you or value your opinion. As noted above, teens generally share parents' values when it comes to views on sexual behavior. One teen who read this book actually told us that she wished her parents were open about talking about this kind of stuff with her; that the fact that they didn't made her feel like she couldn't bring it up.

Telling stories works, especially when it is about something humorous: you can tell stories of what grandma and grandpa said to you when you were a teenager and how embarrassing it was but how you came to realize that they were right. You can invite your teen to share stories about what their peers are talking about or doing. They may not talk to you directly about topics that affect them, but indirect conversations about their grandparents or peers may lay the groundwork for them to discuss their own issues or concerns down the road.

If your teen speaks to you only in monosyllables, you can text them links to articles that you feel speak to important topics. We all have family members who send us "important articles" we have to read, and while we generally hate it, we read them. It may not change our minds, but we do think about them a little. This may be enough for teens to start considering alternatives. Nothing is worse than the parental lecture—but they do listen to what we are saying even if they do not always acknowledge it.

Should I be looking at my children's online communications?

We will be talking more in depth about Internet safety in Chapter 7. However, communication is a key factor in maintaining the rules that you establish with your children. You need to explain early on why rules have been put in place and the reasons behind these rules should be reiterated periodically. You (and your children) may feel like you're invading their privacy (similar to reading their diary) by monitoring their online activity, but communicating with them about the potential dangers of the online world can help them understand why these rules are in place. Thus, having open communication about what you will and will not be monitoring online will be an important foundation for Internet safety.

My child is about to head off to college—how do we continue talking about these topics?

The move to college is a big one for everyone involved. There are new challenges and potential dangers. The CDC estimates that one in five women will be the victim of a sexual assault or an attempted sexual assault during her college career.[51] What makes

---

51 Dills, J., D. Fowler, and G. Payne. 2016. *Sexual Violence on Campus: Strategies for Prevention*. Atlanta, GA: National Center for Injury Prevention and Control, Centers for Disease Control and Prevention, 2016.

it more confusing is that nine out of ten assaults are perpetrated by someone known to the victim, such as a friend, boyfriend, or acquaintance. Although your communications with your child in college will largely be via phone, text, or e-mail, it is important to check in with them regularly. Talk to your college-aged students about the dangers that may be different in college—especially with the presence of alcohol. Boys should also be included in these conversations as well, since they, too, can be victims of sexual violence. You want to make sure that your sons, as well as your daughters, know how to safely handle sexual situations, help someone in distress, and send a positive message about healthy and consensual sexuality.

Take Home Message:
Communication between parent and child is integral to sexual violence prevention. While many schools do some sort of education, this education happens infrequently, and in many cases children forget. It is up to us as parents to make sure that our children have the information they need and that we as community members work together to keep them safe. Keep talking to your children on a regular basis, and these conversations will shift in form and function as your children grow. You will have to be innovative in communicating with them, but do not give up, as they want your advice and feedback even if they do not say so.

Box 6:

Resources for Improving Parent–Child Communications

- Centers for Disease Control and Prevention, Positive Parenting Practices. www.cdc.gov/healthyyouth/protective/positive-parenting/
- Centers for Disease Control and Prevention, Teen Pregnancy: Parent and Guardian Resources. www.cdc.gov/teenpregnancy/parents.htm
- Office of Adolescent Health, Raising Healthy Kids: An Asset-Based Check-in For Parents. www.hhs.gov/ash/oah/resources-and-publications/info/parents/get-started/quiz.html
- Advocates for Youth, Parent-child communication: Promoting sexually healthy youth. www.advocatesforyouth.org/the-facts-parent-child-communication
- The National Campaign to Prevent Teen and Unplanned Pregnancy, Parent-adolescent communication about sex in Latino families: a guide for practitioners. thenationalcampaign.org/resource/parent-adolescent-communication-about-sex-latino-families
- US Department of Health and Human Services, Healthfinder.gov. Talk to Your Kids about Sex www.healthfinder.gov/HealthTopics/Category/parenting/healthy-communication-and-relationships/talk-to-your-kids-about-sex

Box 7: What Topics to Discuss at What Age

Age	What to Discuss
2–3	Begin using accurate names for body parts (penis/vagina).
3–5	Start talking to children about private parts and tell them that no one should be touching those parts.
5–8	Continue earlier conversations, be open about sexuality, and answer children's questions about how babies are made honestly.
8–12	Start discussions of online safety.
12–14	Continue to talk about dangers online, including social media (e.g., SnapChat, Instagram, Facebook) with permission. Begin talking about respect and values in relationships. Begin talking about sexuality and share your values with your children. Answer all biological/anatomical questions honestly.
14–18	Continue previous conversations. Have more specific conversations about parties, dangers of alcohol, and preparation for college life. Discuss consent.
18+	Your child is now technically an adult. This doesn't mean that they do not need you. While there is a fine line between nagging and providing information, they do hear what you say. Let them know you are always a phone call or text away to help and listen to them.

CHAPTER 6

Whom Can I Trust?

As mothers, we can attest that one of the hardest things about parenting is relinquishing control. We want to protect our children from harm. We start out by putting mittens on our newborn babies' hands to keep them from scratching themselves and we graduate to giving our adolescents midnight curfews and monitoring their use of social media. Our role is one of guidance and protection. While things as ordinary as the corners of a coffee table cause danger for very young children, the dangers become more nebulous—more uncertain—as children grow older and venture out independently into the world. While we do what we can to protect our children, we cannot be with them at all times. As they grow, they are increasingly in the company, care, and custody of others. In this chapter, we want to talk about the risks of relinquishing control of our children and how to know whom we can trust.

Being worried about your child is not uncommon. Nor is it unexpected. We hear about child abductions on the news. We receive AMBER Alerts[52] through Facebook and our phones. We

---

52 The AMBER Alert™ Program is a voluntary partnership between law-enforcement agencies, broadcasters, transportation agencies, and the wireless industry to activate an urgent bulletin in the most serious child-abduction cases. Visit www.amberalert.gov/ for more information.

read reports of priests, teachers, and other respected community members abusing children. You might have even received a letter in your mailbox alerting you to a registered sex offender in your neighborhood. So what do we do? We organize playdates, prohibit men who are unaccompanied by children from entering playgrounds, and balk at the idea of our children wandering the neighborhood alone. But is our world really such an unsafe place? Thankfully, it is not. In fact, at least when it comes to sex crimes, the world is arguably a much safer place than it was when you were a kid. Despite popular belief about the rates of sexual offenses, sexual crimes have been on the decline for around the last two decades, with rates of sexual assault falling by more than half since 1995.[53] Rates of violence as a whole have decreased, too. Though we wistfully imagine life in earlier generations to be a place where kids roamed the neighborhood and where parents could be free of worry, the world is, in fact, safer now. People are simply more aware of sexual abuse. It has, in a sense, come out from its place of hiding. The only thing that has really changed is *us*. Our awareness is up—which is great—but along with this heightened awareness comes new anxiety. An exaggerated anxiety, one that leaves us constantly worried about our children's safety and, consequently, has left children without the opportunity to navigate their world freely and independently. Indeed, it's not just that our fears have paralyzed us, but that our efforts to obliterate any and all risk in the lives of our children may inadvertently hinder their attempts to seek out new experiences and test their new abilities.

---

53 Planty, M., L. Langton, C. Krebs, M. Berzofsky, and H. Smiley-McDonald. 2016. *Female victims of sexual violence, 1994–2010*. Washington, DC: Bureau of Justice Statistics, 2016.

So how can we give children the independence that is so vital to their development and yet still ensure their safety?
Striking the right balance is never easy, but as a general rule, we want to encourage you to give your child age-appropriate freedoms. If you are reading this book, you may be among the guilty! While seeking out this book is no doubt a sign of your careful parenting, you are likely to be someone who errs on the side of caution when it comes to your child. This is not bad, but remember that overprotection can be detrimental.[54] Extending trust from an early age allows children to navigate situations, test their abilities and instincts, and learn how to plan, organize, and carry out activities. Let your child speak to the cashier in the grocery store. Have them order their own meal in a restaurant. Encourage them to resolve fights or negotiate dilemmas with their siblings or friends on their own. When they're old enough, give them graduated freedoms. For example, let your child walk to the park with a friend, and later, let them walk to the store or school alone. Your constant presence—while well meaning—can undermine your child's self-confidence and sense of resilience. By hovering, you deprive them of the opportunity to figure things out on their own and undermine their ability to manage increasingly complex social situations. Your first goal, then, should be to work on you. You will find that these graduated freedoms will help instill confidence not only in your child, but also in yourself in terms of your belief that your child will be okay without you.

In Chapter 2, we told you the story of Patty Wetterling. After her son Jacob was abducted in 1989, Patty pushed for a registration law for sex offenders in Minnesota. However, since that time

---

54 Thomasgard, M., W. P. Metz, C. Edelbrock, and J. P. Shonkoff. 1995. Parent-child relationship disorders. Part I. Parental overprotection and the development of the Parent Protection Scale. *Developmental and Behavioral Pediatrics* 16(4): 244–50.

she had a change of heart. When it comes to the lives of children, what does Patty aim for now? You might be surprised to learn that she encourages us to abandon our exaggerated fears and to try to live in the kind of world we lived in before, a world where we gave children more freedoms—the world that existed before Jacob was abducted. She encourages parents *not* to become more vigilant or fearful, but rather to be alive in the world—to eat ice cream with their kids, to play with their children, and to help their neighbors (see "In the Dark" podcast, an in-depth investigation into the Jacob Wetterling case[55]). Being immersed in data and the discussion of sex offender policies, Patty learned that much of what we are doing to protect children is not working. Basing our policy on "stranger danger" type assumptions doesn't keep us any safer, it only serves to reinforce the misconceptions that we have about the nature of sexual violence.

Should I still be teaching my kids not to get into cars with strangers?

Yes. Though a small and statistically rare risk, these kinds of things do happen. As you learned in Chapter 1, some 7 percent of sex offenses against children are committed by strangers. Make sure your child knows that they should never go off anywhere with someone they don't know, regardless of whether that person knows their name, says they know their parents, incentivizes them in some way (e.g., offers a puppy or an ice-cream cone), or threatens them with harm if they do not obey. Teach your kid about safe strangers—people like police officers, school teachers, other parents in the park—who they can go to if they need help. Children should also know to be wary of a stranger who asks for help. When an adult really needs assistance with something, they ask another adult—not a child.

---

55 American Public Media Reports. October 4, 2016. Season 1, Episode 6: Stranger Danger. Available at http://www.apmreports.org/in-the-dark.

Encourage them to trust their own instincts and work to develop their self-confidence. Kids who are assertive and display self-confidence are at an advantage. An abuser will look for the path of least resistance and thus avoid a child who knows his or her rights and asserts him or herself, as these children may be more likely to alert someone, put up a struggle, or otherwise make the task of leading them away from the rest of the crowd more difficult. So while you should remember that these kinds of stranger abductions are exceptionally rare, being prepared for the unexpected and unlikely is still a good idea.

What should I do if someone gives me a bad feeling?

Just as we encourage children to trust their instincts, we hope you will trust your own, too. If your new neighbors make you feel uneasy, avoid leaving your child alone with them. Err on the side of caution if someone gives you a bad feeling. But remember, people who prey on children may look a lot different from the idea of sexual predators that we have in our heads. Child abusers are not always the creepy strangers we see in the movies or in the cases that make headlines on TV. They can be pillars of the community—doctors, lawyers, clergy members—who are socially adept and likable and who charm their ways into our lives. They can be uncles and aunts, brothers, sisters, cousins, stepparents, or dads or mothers—people whom we know and love and invite into our homes without hesitation. Additionally, about one-third of all child molestation is perpetrated by other children below the age of eighteen.[56] Indeed, the school friends of your child, neighborhood kids, or peer-age relatives are responsible for a sizeable portion of abuse that occurs. Children below the age of eighteen still lack a fully developed prefrontal cortex, and adolescents often struggle with sexual urges. Because the frontal cortex

---

56 Stop It Now! 2007. Do children sexually abuse other children? Retrieved from https://www.safersociety.org/uploads/WP075-DoChildren.pdf.

affects judgment and risk-taking behavior, youth can be particularly likely to act on urges or make bad decisions.

So instead of focusing on someone's appearance or role in the community, focus on habits or actions. For example, while many of us might be quick to be suspicious of the socially awkward neighbor who lives alone but not the charming doctor who is liked by everyone, habits may be more revealing. Be wary of people who encourage secrets. Be careful with someone who abuses alcohol or other substances that impair judgment and lower inhibitions. Be alert when someone wants to spend increasing amounts of time alone with your child. Be watchful of someone who themselves seems childlike in their ways or tends to engage children in physical play, like roughhousing or tickling, as emotional identification with children is a risk factor for abuse, and desensitizing a child to touch may be a grooming strategy. Pay attention to changes in your child's behavior as well. If their behavior or mood begins to abruptly change in some concerning way, you might give thought as to who they have been spending time with and what might be going on.

Should I leave my child alone with my new boyfriend?

This is a question that is probably not asked enough. One of the things we observed in our research is that parents can be very— perhaps overly—paranoid about the risk of "stranger danger" type crimes and yet not be aware that someone close to them could commit abuse. Data from the US Department of Health and Human Services reveal that stepfathers, adoptive fathers, and boyfriends show disproportionately higher rates of sexual abuse than do biological fathers, especially against girls.[57]

---

57 US Department for Health and Human Services Office of the Assistant Secretary for Planning and Evaluation. 2005. Male perpetrators of child maltreatment: Findings from NCANDS. Retrieved from https://aspe.hhs.gov/basic-report/male-perpetrators-child-maltreatment-findings-ncands#Key.

Certainly not everyone is a dangerous predator, and if you are a parent who is venturing out into the dating world again, we don't want to scare you. But being measured and careful in your decisions is wise. There is data to support the old adage that love is blind. Research has shown that the brains of people who are in love look unique in terms of neurochemical activity. Brain levels of cortisol, oxytocin, and dopamine may rise, and research shows that "when we are engaged in romantic love, the neural machinery responsible for making critical assessments of other people, including assessments of those with whom we are romantically involved, shuts down."[58] We are more willing to overlook a red flag when hopeful about a new relationship or when we are in the throes of new love. Sometimes, especially after a failed relationship or another life crisis, we are so desperate to have success that we excuse troubling behaviors. Or we may simply rush into things, "playing house" with someone before we've really gotten a chance to know them well. Take your time, get to know your new partner well, and no matter how in love or how much you'd like for this relationship to be "the one," stay alert for red flags. You should be especially wary if your children ask you not to leave them alone with your boyfriend—this suggests that something is amiss, and you need to talk to them about it.

In rare cases, you may meet someone who confesses to a past crime or tells you that they are on a sex offender registry. Remember: excuses and minimizations are very common among offenders. Seldom in these situations do offenders tell you the unflattering and incriminatory details of their crimes. More likely is a well-crafted story about how the child was coached to say abuse was happening or an ex-wife was out to get him in front of the

---

58 Harvard Medical School Department of Neurobiology. *Love and the brain.* The Harvard Mahoney Neuroscience Institute Letter. Retrieved from http://neuro.hms.harvard.edu/harvard-mahoney-neuroscience-institute/brain-newsletter/and-brain-series/love-and-brain.

court or simply how the details add up to something other than a sexual offense. As learned in Chapter 1, we know that most sex offenders do not reoffend, but we also know that the best predictor of future behavior is past behavior. Thus it is always prudent *not* to leave your child unsupervised around someone who has committed a sexual offense.

What about leaving my child alone with a karate coach, piano teacher, or others who give private lessons?

Again, caution should be exercised here. If you are contracting somehow outside of a school or institution, it's unlikely that they'll have been subjected to any kind of formal background check. So you may want to be more vigilant here and check their references. Talk to other parents who have used their service or ask to sit in during a lesson. Is it the type of environment where parents are encouraged to be active and involved, or does your presence seem to be unwelcome? Take note of the surroundings. Are there windowed areas through which you can observe your child? Are there other people present, and do they have a direct line of sight to where the classes are taking place?

Above all, as we will stress in later chapters, make sure to maintain open lines of communication with your child and observe behavior. Talk to them about their lessons and how they feel about their coach or teacher. Listen to your child if they tell you they want to stop lessons—figure out if it is because their teacher makes them feel uncomfortable. Here is where it is important to trust your child's instincts. If regular and open communication is the norm in your family, your child will be more likely to open up if something is making them uncomfortable.

How do I find a babysitter whom I can trust?

One strategy is to use a sitter who is connected through an organization, i.e., someone at your state-run school or licensed day care facility. In this case, you can ask someone at the organization whether they screen their employees and what the screening involves. You can also ask how long that person has worked there and ask for permission to inquire about their employee record. Knowing that someone has been at a facility for ten years without incident would, for us, instill a great deal of confidence. If, however, you are going to contract a babysitter on your own, then the work of doing a background check rests with you. Many online sites will allow you to do a background search for a small fee. Also, be sure to get references and contacts for these individuals. You may want to have a session where they watch your children when you are home so you can see how they interact with them. In addition, most home alarm companies now have live streaming options that can be set up in common areas so that you can monitor what is going on in the home when you are not there. Even if you do not regularly check, this extra level of vigilance may be enough to prevent any abuse from happening. As always, listen to your children. If your children ask you not to leave them alone with the babysitter, find out why and what is going on.

Many of us feel safer since babysitters are usually women; however, women can also sexually abuse children. While statistics show that females commit far fewer offenses than males, these types of offenses are often not identified or go unreported, making our knowledge about sex offenses committed by females incomplete.

Can I trust those who work at schools, day care centers, or churches?

We bestow our trust on individuals who work with children—teachers, childcare workers, clergy, doctors, and others who come into contact with our children in institutional settings. Due to the trust granted to them and the authority they hold that children must respect, these community pillars sometimes abuse this trust to access children.[59] Most employees of schools or licensed day care centers go through some sort of employment screening, and many states require teachers to undergo criminal background checks as well as child abuse background checks prior to hiring. That said, caution must still be exercised. Sometimes people who have not yet offended, or who have not yet been caught, may slip through. It is equally important to pay attention to the policies and procedures of the school. Do they have open-door policies? Are there clear reporting structures if something takes place? Are your concerns here as a parent taken seriously? One of the things that investigations into the Catholic Church sexual abuse scandal revealed was that the culture or the institution can facilitate or hinder abuse. Institutions concerned with tarnishing their image, for example, sometimes seek to push reports under the rug or look the other way when it comes to concerning behavior. These types of environments are precisely those in which abuse thrives. The Catholic Church now requires all employees to complete Safe Environment Training, which encourages reporting of suspicious behavior, establishes clear rules for adult-child interactions, alerts adults to warning signs for abuse, and includes pre-employment screening of employees.[60]

Should I allow my child to have sleepovers?

59 Falkenbach, D., A. Foehse, E. Jeglic, C. Calkins, and L. Raymaekers. 2017. Sexual abuse within employment settings–A comparison of work-related, intra- and extra-familial child molesters. *Sexual Abuse: A Journal of Research and Treatment* (June 1, 2017). doi: 10.1177/1079063217708202. [Remember to preserve italics for the title "Sexual Abuse..."]

60 Desai, K. and D. Lew. 2012. Safe environment training: The effectiveness of the Catholic Church's child sexual abuse prevention programs. Houston, TX: Children at Risk Institute.

This is a very personal decision, and as a parent you should do what makes you feel comfortable. If you choose to allow your child to stay overnight with a friend, try and get to know the family or the environment. Have you been in the home? Do you know their habits and rules? Are there other people dropping in at all hours? As mentioned earlier, we encourage you to give your child age-appropriate independence. Being overly distrustful is not healthy and sends a fear-filled message to your child that the world is a dangerous place. Provide loving instruction and give them the opportunity to function in a new environment; an environment where the food, rules, and customs are different will open your child's mind and allow them to practice and develop their independence. However, when leaving your child anywhere for any prolonged period of time you should know where they are, who they are with, and who else will be there. Always, of course, make sure your child has a way to contact you should they feel uncomfortable for any reason.

Should I allow my child to go to overnight camp?

Just as with deciding whether to allow your child to have sleepovers, deciding whether your child can go to an overnight camp is a choice some parents are more comfortable with than others. If you decide to do so, look up the camp on the Better Business Bureau. Ask whether employees are screened. Do a Google or Yelp search to find out what other families' experiences have been. Visit the camp ahead of time and speak with the camp director. Ideally, send your child to an overnight camp with a friend, as there is power in numbers and children are less likely to be targeted if they are seen as being part of a group as opposed to being alone.[61]

---

61 Winters, G. M., and E. L. Jeglic. 2016. Stages of Sexual grooming: Recognizing potentially predatory behaviors of child molesters. *Deviant Behavior* 38(6): 724-33. doi:10.1080/01639625.2016.1197656.

Maybe I should just keep my kid within arm's reach at all times?

No. Remember that teaching kids to live in a dangerous world—a world where they will fall off of a bike and make mistakes—is part of what helps them grow. While we have tried to set parameters and provide some things to think about, you don't want your children to grow up in a world where you are nervously ticking off checklists prior to every encounter they have. Letting your children test their independence and develop age-appropriate skills will instill confidence, hone their sense of judgment, and ultimately help to keep them safer in the world.

Take Home Message:

What we hope you have learned in this chapter is that the risk of sexual assault is probably much less than you have assumed. The good news is that your children are probably much safer than you think, and they are much safer than children were just a few decades ago. Giving them age-appropriate freedoms is encouraged. But still, always do your due diligence—do background checks where feasible, be vigilant, stay alert for red flags or things that make you feel uneasy (including non-verbal cues), and, above all, trust your own instincts and those of your child.

Box 8

The Archdiocese of Philadelphia, once embroiled in the clergy sexual abuse scandal, now delivers Safe Environment Training initiated by the US Conference on Catholic Bishops as part of their response to the abuse crisis. The Archdiocese of Philadelphia alone has trained over sixty thousand employees and volunteers. Among the skills taught is the recognition of signs of abuse, which the Archdiocese website lists as follows:

- Recurring nightmares
- Insomnia or increased sleeping
- Sudden regressive behavior
- Fear of the dark
- Withdrawal from others
- Aggressive behavior
- Change in performance at school
- Loss of self-esteem
- Poor self-image
- Deteriorating peer relationships (loss of interest in friends)
- Loss of interest in enjoyable activities

Though you should remember that any one of these signs (e.g., fear of the dark) are common in children, if you begin to see a pattern of multiple signs, this may signal that something is going on with your child. Whether or not it is abuse, you should pursue this by talking to a health care professional or mental health provider.

Archdiocese of Philadelphia Office for Child and Youth Protection. 2009. Safe Environment Program. Retrieved from http://archphila.org/prevention/Safe%20Environment42009.pdf

CHAPTER 7

What to Know about Dangers Online

Just several decades back, people (including us!) grew up without cell phones and Internet access. Perhaps life was simpler then— or at the very least, our parents did not have to worry about our online safety. While connection to the Internet through our innumerable devices has many benefits, it can bring with it a host of dangers—the biggest of those dangers being the risk of online solicitation of our children by sexual offenders. This chapter will review what we know about those who use the Internet to offend against children and what we as parents can do to protect our children so they can safely use the Internet, whether for school work, play, or just exploration.

What dangers exist online?
The Internet gives us the world at our fingertips from the comfort of our home. While this is wonderful in many ways, it can also bring dangers into the home that we do not anticipate. Even as we warn our children about strangers in their physical environment, many of us fail to think of the various ways in which our children can come into contact with strangers on the Internet. Although the majority of people they communicate

with will not have any malicious intent, there are some who will.

Many of us became aware of online dangers after the show *To Catch a Predator* aired on television in 2004. In this reality-based show, undercover police officers posed as children in online forums and engaged in chat room conversations and other Internet-based message groups. In some of these cases, online sexual offenders contacted and made arrangements to meet the "children" in person; and when they did, they were met not with children but instead with police and cameras.

In 1985, a federal law made it illegal to communicate with children via mail (or any other manner, which broadly encompassed the Internet) with the intent of luring a minor to engage in sexual activity. This was followed in 1996 by the Telecommunications Act, which specifically applied this restriction to the Internet and online communications, including the transmission of sexual pictures or luring minors to engage in online sexual behavior.[62] Thus, any online communication between an adult and your child in which sexual language, images, or behaviors are discussed or exchanged is breaking the law. What makes this difficult to monitor and prosecute, however, is the global nature of Internet communications. Different countries have different laws, and what is illegal in one place may not be illegal in another. Additionally, different countries have different priorities (whether they consider this type of crime to be a priority), resources (whether they have the money and technological resources to devote to prosecutions), and jurisdictions (whether they have the proper legal standing), which complicate the process of identifying and prosecuting offenders. Fortunately, prosecution of these online offenders is a global priority, and there are

---

62 Seto, M. C. 2013. *Internet Sex Offenders*. Washington, DC: American Psychological Association, 2013.

international organizations, such as the Global Virtual Taskforce, that work with government and private organizations to detect and prosecute online offenders. However, many online predators are skilled and have ways of covering up their identities and locations. So even when we know this is going on, we may not be able to apprehend them. Thus, it is primarily up to us as parents to make sure our children do not get lured into inappropriate communications with someone they know or don't know.

The most recent estimates are that approximately one in seven children/teenagers receive some sort of unwanted sexual solicitation online.[63] While girls are more frequently targeted than boys, about 25 percent of those who have been victims of Internet-initiated sex crimes are boys. Boys have been found to be particularly vulnerable if they are gay or questioning their sexual identity, with studies showing that many contacts are made in LGBTQ-oriented chat rooms.[64]

While we think of these online predators as strangers, there is evidence that a significant number of the individuals who have been arrested for online sex crimes are family and friends of the victim. One study found that 18 percent of the arrests for online sexual crimes in the US over a one-year period were family and friends of the victims.[65] In about two-thirds of these cases, online communication was being used to seduce and groom the victims through sharing of sexual pictures and/or discussion of sexual acts.

63 Wolak, J., K. Mitchell, and D. Finkelhor. 2006. Online victimization: 5 years later. Alexandria, VA: National Center for Missing & Exploited Children. Available at: http://www.unh.edu/ccrc/pdf/CV138.pdf.

64 Wolak, J., D. Finkelhor, and K. Mitchell. 2004. Internet-initiated sex crimes against minors: Implications for prevention based on findings from a national study. *Journal of Adolescent Health* 35(5): 424.e11-424.e20. doi: http://dx.doi.org/10.1016/j.jadohealth.2004.05.006.

65 Mitchell, K. J., D. Finkelhor, and J. Wolak. 2005. The internet and family and acquaintance sexual abuse. *Child Maltreatment* 10(1): 49–60.

What makes this type of crime particularly concerning is that in almost all the cases, the children/teenagers meet with the sexual offender willingly, and they agreed to meet them in-person knowing that they would be engaging in some sort of sexual activity. As troubling as this is, however, it gives us avenues for prevention. Educating our children about these tactics and dynamics can help to prevent these contacts and interactions from happening in the first place.

Who are online predators?

As with most sex offenders, there is no particular profile of Internet sex offenders. In many cases, they are well-respected members of the community. In one study, 99 percent of all Internet offenders were male, with the majority (76 percent) being older than twenty-six years of age.[3] Almost half were over twenty years older than their victims. These individuals are generally attracted to adolescents (as opposed to young children), and their primary targets are usually teens, aged thirteen to seventeen years old, whom they target in chat rooms and online platforms that cater primarily to youth, geographic locations, and dating/romance. As mentioned above, in about one out of five cases, the perpetrator is a family member or friend who is using the Internet as a way to groom or seduce the child/teen for sexual contact.

How do online predators target children?

Since the Jerry Sandusky case at Pennsylvania State University in 2011, many of us have become familiar with the term "sexual grooming." This occurs when sex offenders develop trusting relationships with a victim in a way that opens the door for abuse to occur without detection. Many Internet offenders use a similar modus operandi (MO), in that they engage in relatively lengthy chats with the potential victim before suggesting that they meet in person. Many of these chats can last weeks or even months before the topic of meeting in person is introduced. These offenders can be quite skilled at saying the right things to children to gain their trust and pique their interest. They are also good at identifying which youth may be more likely to meet them by looking for those with pictures in their profiles or those with racier screen names, such as hotsexymamma69 or ready-togo.[66]

Individuals who commit online crimes know how to target the children and teenagers who are most vulnerable. They often lurk in chat rooms and observe interactions before reaching out. One study found that children who were victimized tended to be female; engaged in more risk-taking and impulsive behaviors; and had low self-esteem, depression, and/or a history of trauma.[67] Another study found that those who had been victims tended to come from troubled homes where there was not a lot of parental oversight.[68] The good news is that these researchers also found that having parental support and high self-esteem often prevented offenders' attempts to groom.

Before meeting in person, many offenders speak on the phone with their potential victim (76 percent) or send them pictures (48 percent) or gifts/money (47 percent). In almost all cases examined in a 2004 study, the teens met with the offenders willingly,

66 Winters, G. M., L. E. Kaylor, and E. L. Jeglic. 2017. Sexual offenders contacting children online: An examination of transcripts of sexual grooming. *Journal of Sexual Aggression* 23(1): 62–76. doi: 10.1080/13552600.2016.1271146.

67 Whittle, H., C. Hamilton-Giachritsis, A. Beech, and G. Collings. 2013. A review of online grooming: Characteristics and concerns. *Aggression and Violent Behavior* 18(1): 62–70.

68 Whittle, H. C., C. E. Hamilton-Giachritsis, and A. R. Beech. 2014. In their own words: Young peoples' vulnerabilities to being groomed and sexually abused online. *Psychology,* 5(10): 1185–96.

and about half of the teens reported being in love or having feelings for the perpetrator before they meet in person.[69]

How can I spot an online predator—do they use false identities?

While very few online predators will give their true name, many will *not* use deception about their age or their motivation. For example, one large-scale research study found that only 5 percent of online sexual offenders pretended to be teenagers.[70] About 25 percent of Internet-based offenders will pretend to be somewhat younger than their true age, but the majority still represent themselves as adults.[69]

About 80 percent of online predators initiated conversation about sex at some point before the in-person meeting, with 20 percent engaging in some type of cybersex and 18 percent sending sexually explicit photographs. Surprisingly, in this study,[69] researchers found that a full 48 percent of all Internet initiated sex offenders did not lie or deceive the adolescent before meeting in person.

Internet safety seems overwhelming to me—where do I start?

To be honest, it *is* a little overwhelming. That is largely because it is a moving target and one that is constantly changing. We may just be getting used to one online platform when our children start to use another one. Also, kids are getting Internet-enabled

---

69 Wolak, J., D. Finkelhor, and K. Mitchel. 2004. Internet-initiated sex crimes against minors: Implications for prevention based on findings from a national study. *Journal of Adolescent Health* 35(5): 424.e11-242.e20.

70 Malesky, L. A. 2007. Predatory online behavior: Modus operandi of convicted sex offenders in identifying potential victims and contacting minors over the Internet. *Journal of Child Sexual Abuse* 16(2): 23–32. doi:10.1300/J070v16n02_02.

devices earlier and earlier. Preschoolers are using iPads and kindles, which are often Internet enabled. In a way, it is kind of analogous to the way that our parents never learned to use the VCR. Even though we may pride ourselves on our social media savvy, our children are probably going to be savvier than we are—and that is just something we have to accept.

However, this is where having those open lines of communication are important. Part of being on top of what our children are doing online is showing interest and asking them about it. If you have this open discourse with your kids, they will be more likely to tell you if they have encountered anything online that has made them uncomfortable. They need to know that they can talk to you, even if they were doing something wrong, such as chatting with a stranger about sex.

How can I monitor what my kids do online?

There are various ways to keep tabs on your children.

- Talk to your child about online dangers. This can be done once your child starts to use the computer/Internet-enabled devices more independently, and the conversation should be age-appropriate. You will want to talk to them about privacy issues, telling them never to identify their name, school, or the city/state in which they live. You should also emphasize that while the Internet is a wonderful resource, there are some people who may use it inappropriately, and if they ever see or experience something that makes them uncomfortable, they should tell or show it to you.
- You need to make family rules about the use of Internet-enabled devices. For example, all Internet-enabled devices must be used in common areas—like the kitchen, den, family room, etc.—where the family congregates. This

enables you to look at your child's screen and see what is being viewed; it also decreases the likelihood that they will access any sites (such as pornography—see Chapter 8 for a discussion of the research on pornography usage by tween/teens) that they are not supposed to. If you do allow your children to use Internet-enabled devices in their rooms (i.e., laptops to do homework) as they get older, it is best to establish ground rules such that these devices are not allowed in rooms after bedtime. Not only will this help them to develop good sleep habits, it also prevents children from accessing the Internet and going online when you are not aware of it.

- Do periodic browser history checks. Most web browsers, such as Internet Explorer, Safari, Google Chrome, or Mozilla Firefox, will allow you to check their browser history to see what websites have been frequented. This will be done following the conversation you have with your tween about expectations for on-line privacy as discussed in Chapter 8. You want to be especially mindful of whether there are any pornography related sites, chat rooms, or social media sites you are unaware of. These sorts of checks should happen every two weeks or so (see Box 9).

- Install software or devices (see next page) that can help you with monitoring and detecting inappropriate online activity.

- Many kids no longer use desktops or tablets and are glued to their smartphones. The same rules apply, and software can also be installed on phones and safeguards put in place to monitor the content they are viewing and the apps they are using.

- Enlist your community. While teens may not always tell their parents what they are doing, they may tell their friends who may in turn tell their parents. If another parent hears from their child that a friend is doing something potentially dangerous online, we need to share that information. There are discussion questions at the end of this book (page 156) that can start these conversations in your communities.

Is there software available to keep my kids safe?

Fortunately for us, the answer to this is a resounding yes! There are in fact innumerable programs and devices out there that can be installed on your computer to monitor what your children are doing and viewing, as well as blocking them from websites that they should not be visiting (e.g., pornography). Depending upon the software or device, you can also expand the coverage to all devices that are Internet enabled, including gaming consoles, smartphones, and tablets. In addition, there is software available to track social media that will alert you when certain words and phrases are mentioned. These devices and software are constantly changing, so the best thing to do is to check out online technology sites (see Box 10) for reviews and features, and use that information to decide what works best for your family's needs.

My kids know so much more about this stuff than I do—how do I keep up?

It is hard to keep up. It feels sometimes like you finally figured out what Snapchat and Vine are, but now everyone is talking about Yik Yak and Tinder. There are websites that review the latest apps and social media platforms so you can see what is out there; you can also use Google with the search words "popular social media platforms," which will list the top hits. Finally—the recurring theme of this book—talk with your child/teen about what new apps or games they are using. Ask them to show them to you, and in many cases, they will likely enjoy talking to you about the latest app, game, or social media platform. Whatever you do, don't put your head in the sand and refuse to learn about the latest fad because it's not what your generation is using. Ask your child about it, read up on it, and maybe even access the app or website yourself.

At what age is it okay for them to have Facebook, Twitter, Instagram, or Snapchat?

Facebook, Twitter, Instagram, and Snapchat all require that users be a minimum of thirteen years old before having an account. Vine, Tinder, and Yik Yak require users to be seventeen years of age, and YouTube requires users to be eighteen years old (however, children can have an account at age thirteen with parental permission). Facebook even has a website where users can report underage users, and, if verified, these accounts will be deleted.

While there are millions of underage users of these social media sites, it is important to teach your children that there are laws of society that have to be followed. If they do set up an account, it means they have lied about their birthdate. This sets a precedent that it is okay to engage in these types of "white lies"— which are precisely the things we are trying to avoid when we keep the lines of communication open. There are many reasons why these age restrictions have been put in place, and supporting or silently condoning their underage social media use sets a poor example of the behaviors and morals we are trying to impart upon them.

Can I friend/follow my teen on social media?

This is a discussion to have with your teenager. Some teenagers feel they want their space/privacy on social media, while others are happy to have their parents as friends. If your child is reluctant to have you as part of their online life, do not insist. If they do let you, do your best to give them some space, observing silently and not commenting on each and every one of their posts or photos. Another option is to have all their online usernames and passwords. This way, you are not watching them on a daily basis, but you have the ability to check and see what is going on if you notice that your child's behavior has changed.

My kids only play games online—they don't use social media—do I have to worry?

Unfortunately, yes—many games these days are interactive, and players all over the world are able to connect to one another and communicate. Parents usually allow younger children to play online games, thinking them to be safe. However, many games today have a "chat" feature where players can communicate with one another. While many of the players just want to comment on the game and strategy, online predators know that these are opportunities for them to get in contact with unsuspecting children. Online predators are known to message child players, asking for their phone numbers so they can text and share pictures. In some cases, they might attempt to meet the child in person.

In order to prevent online communication with adults, only allow younger children to play games that do not have chat features. Talk to your children about using screen names that do not reveal their identity (name and image) or location. Also tell your children that they should never give identifying information (name, location, e-mail, cell phone number) or share photographs or videos with anyone they communicate with online. They should be taught to tell you if anyone tries to get this information from them.

Take Home Message:

The Internet is a wonderful resource for children and teens, not only as a source of information but also as a way to connect with their peers. However, the Internet also brings with it a host of dangers. As parents, we have to know and understand these dangers. We have to keep up and do our research, and while it can seem overwhelming, fortunately we also have the Internet at our fingertips to help educate us. We have to talk to our children about these dangers as they start to explore the Internet, but ultimately it is our responsibility to monitor their online behavior and contacts. Luckily, there are various software and devices that can assist us. Finally, the best way to prevent your child from succumbing to online dangers is to talk with them and keep the lines of communication open.

Box 9: How to Check Browser History

Google Chrome: Press **Ctrl + H** to view browsing history.
Firefox: Press **Ctrl + H;** the browsing history will appear on the left.
Internet Explorer 11: Click the star-shaped **Favorites** button at the top-right of its window → When textbox opens, click on **History.**

Box 10

A recent study surveyed a large sample of young adults and asked about their experiences chatting online as children and adolescents. Out of 374 participants, 30 percent reported that they had chatted with adult strangers online when they were below the age of eighteen. Of those who chatted with adult strangers, 66 percent recalled receiving some form of sexual solicitation from an adult, which often included requests for sexual pictures, conversations about sexual history, or sexual flattery. Around 53 percent of kids who chatted with adult strangers recalled having a relationship of sorts, in that they considered the other person to be a romantic partner, and 12 percent actually met with an adult stranger from an Internet chat room to have sexual intercourse. Overall, the young adults surveyed in this study reported minimal negative consequences related to having an online relationship and offline sexual contact with an adult stranger, suggesting that children may perceive online romance with adults to be a legitimate and consensual relationship despite differences in age. These findings emphasize the necessity for parents to keep open lines of communication about what sites children are accessing online and especially with whom they are talking online.

Greene-Colozzi, E. 2017. An exploration of youth experiences in chatrooms. Unpublished master's thesis. John Jay College of Criminal Justice.

Box 11: Websites that Review Internet Monitoring Apps for Computers and Smartphones

Pcmag.com

Toptenreviews.com

Techradar.com

Digitaltrends.com

Tomsguide.com

Topsoftwarereviews.net

Teaching kids about online safety: Google's Be Internet Awesome campaign provides parents, teachers, and kids with interactive lessons on how to stay safe online. It includes an adventure-style computer game that teaches children the fundamentals of digital safety: beinternetawesome.withgoogle.com/

CHAPTER 8

Talking to Your Pre-Teen

Awkward. Dreaded. Uncomfortable. These are the types of words we often use to describe the sex talk that happens between a mom or a dad and their child. These words apply as much to the parent's delivery of the talk as to the child's receipt of it. We might not want to have the talk any more than they want to hear it. So notoriously uncomfortable are these "birds and the bees" discussions that they make the stuff of Hollywood comedies. But does it have to be this way? No. And we hope that, after reading this chapter, you'll think a little differently about how you approach these talks.

We're not going to give you a pass on having the talk, but we are going to ask you to consider a new perspective. We hope to make these discussions easier on you, in turn ensuring that your child will also be made more comfortable, allowing him or her to hear this information better.

In this chapter, we will focus specifically on your pre-teen (i.e., "tween") child—that age between childhood and adolescence—often thought of as between eight and fourteen years of age. You may wonder how to talk about serious matters with a pre-teen, a person who is increasingly asserting their autonomy and who may find your very presence to be embarrassing. But it is precisely this stage of newfound independence and exploration that makes talks about sex generally—and sexual danger specifically—critical.

When, where, and how should I have the "sex talk"?

There is no precise age at which you should have "the talk." In fact, if you are thinking about it as a single talk that you will have at a certain age and place, you are thinking about this wrong. The sex talks (plural!) that will happen with your pre-adolescent are really nothing more than a continuation of the talks that you've already begun. By now, you will hopefully have set a foundation by using the correct labels for body parts and perhaps providing rudimentary information on how babies are born and other low-stakes kinds of questions. Your tween, however, is more curious about sex and will have more sophisticated questions. You will need to up your game. Explaining that boys have a penis and girls don't will now be replaced with talk about the physiology of how erections occur and more philosophical discussions that frame matters such as sexual consent. So how do you do this?

The sex talk of Hollywood lore often happens in a bedroom, with the mother or father sitting down at a pivotal point in childhood to deliver a stiff lecture about the birds and the bees. We want to encourage you to find a place—or places—that are natural and comfortable for you. If you are often in your child's bedroom sitting on their bed and discussing topics, then by all means have discussions about sex in that same environment. But if you find that your most meaningful discussions happen when you're in the car together or running errands, then have the discussion in that environment.

Maybe you take walks with your child or have a special activity that only the two of you do together. Setting aside one-on-one time for your child regularly—time where you can do something together without the distraction of phones, work, or other siblings—helps to give your child the individualized attention they crave from parents and also provides a natural environment that promotes these sorts of discussions. Set good parenting practices in place and start having that one-on-one time now, so that no matter the questions, concerns, or fears that your child has down the road, they know that they have a safe time and place to discuss these issues with you.

Using a conversation starter is also recommended. Perhaps the book your child is reading or something you both saw on the news can serve an impetus to the discussion. Is the character in your child's novel struggling with newfound sexual feelings? Was there a report of a local rape on the morning news? Is there talk of a local LGBTQ Pride event happening in your community? Maybe you overheard one of their friends at sports practice making a comment about a "blow job." Whatever it is, we encourage you to seize the moment to bring up conversations around sex. Just as these discussions shouldn't happen just one time in childhood, they also shouldn't be solely about the mechanics of sex or physical changes brought on by puberty. This is your opportunity to talk to your child about other things and bigger issues that are important to sexual relations: sexual orientation and gender identity; offering and receiving consent; safe sex practices; peer pressure and bullying; intimacy and respect; and/or patriarchal attitudes and sexist comments. Remember that sexual offenses do not happen in a vacuum. In many ways they reflect the attitudes, norms, and culturally accepted practices of our society.

Also know that a long, lengthy discussion will probably not be well received. Again, it's best to think about this not as "the" sex talk, but rather as one of many short discussions you will have with your kids throughout their childhood. Their brains have a lot to process. Think about your first day on a job. Someone probably showed you around, gave you a bunch of paperwork to fill out, and explained a lot of things at once. You likely had to ask someone to remind you of the most basic things, like where the bathroom is located, and you probably also felt that you forgot half of what you learned that first day. With information overload, we end up forgetting much of what we learn. But brief discussions here and there allow our children to absorb and process the information. So seize the moment when the opportunity arises, have a brief discussion, and then move on. Go back to talking about soccer or swim practice or whatever you normally talk about with your child when you're in the car or picking up a pizza. Go back to checking out new books in the library or kicking the ball around together. Again, the take home message here is that it is not one and done, but rather an ongoing conversation. It may be one minute here and another few minutes there, but you have now demonstrated to your child that you are open to talking about these topics—you are not embarrassed by them, they can come to you with any of their questions and concerns, and you will take them seriously.

What does your tween child need to know about sex at this point?

It is at this point in their development when kids' bodies start to change. Going through puberty brings the coarsening and growth of pubic hair, the enlargement of the testes and lengthening of the penis, and the development of breast buds and enlargement of areolae. It is at this stage that girls will begin menstruating and boys may begin to have more spontaneous erections. Though most children at this age are not yet having sex, it's not too early to begin discussing it. Curiosity about sex is normal, and to the extent that you can create an environment for healthy open discussions, your children will be more likely to come to you for questions or to disclose what's going on in their lives. Remember that our own tone in these discussions sets lifelong patterns in place for how children think about sex. Avoid over-reaction, secrecy, and shame. If you dismiss their feelings or send subtle messages that we shouldn't talk about these kinds of things or have these kinds of feelings, your child might be less likely to come talk to you when they are in trouble.

If you tell them stuff they already know, they will probably see you as out of touch. But if you are overwhelming them with technical details beyond their developmental level, you will rapidly lose their interest. So how then to find the sweet spot of age-appropriate sex talk? Try to get a gauge on where your child is. What things have they heard friends talking about? What kinds of sexual situations has he or she encountered on TV? What bigger social issues are happening in the world around you? Use this information to gauge your own discussion and also to clarify any misconceptions that they have. And don't forget to ask them! Do you know about this already? Is this confusing? No one can gauge better than your child regarding where they are at in terms of their knowledge and curiosity.

When you begin discussions with your pre-teen, first and foremost, you want to normalize sexual feelings and curiosities. Often kids feel like they are the only one to have struggled with something, whether it is worrying about getting their period, having gotten an erection in class, struggling with same-sex sexual feelings, or being body shamed by one of their peers. If this is a struggle that you have shared, let your child know your experience. If you are uncomfortable sharing your personal experiences, you can talk about how one of your friends was struggling with something similar at your child's age and how that was handled. If it was handled poorly, it is a good time to ask your child for how such a situation could have been handled differently. If you cannot come up with any examples yourself, then help them to find solutions to their problems by locating resources or seeking help. Your library can be a great resource.

It is also important to set limits. Children at this age want to explore and to figure things out, but they also need rules and limits. Make sure they are aware of rules in your house with regard to TV and movies (e.g., are PG-13 movies allowed?), social media access (e.g., can they have an Instagram account?), friendships (are they allowed to close the door to their room when friends are over?), clothing (are any types of clothing not allowed by your school district or in your family?), etc. Make sure they know that smartphones and social media are a privilege, not a right. Ground rules for use should be established, and a clear message should be given that violation of those rules will result in suspension of those privileges.

As researchers in the area of sexual violence prevention, we consider the discussion of sex to be much bigger than just the mechanics of sex, reproduction, and puberty. Keeping your child safe is also about instilling a value system. If they learn about respectful behavior and see it modeled in their home, they will be less likely to accept sexually inappropriate behavior as normal. For example, some parents keep secrets from one another in the form of "Don't tell Dad that we stopped for ice cream." But the implicit message here is that secrecy is okay in the family. And when secrecy is okay, children will be less likely to question an abuser who encourages them not to tell anyone. Likewise, children are keen observers of the behavior they see in the home. If you listen to your partner and treat them respectfully—regardless of whether you agree or disagree—children will see this. And they will learn that their home is a place where issues or concerns can be raised and where disagreements are handled with respect.

What should I say/do if they stumble onto online pornography?

Children are curious by nature, and nothing makes us more curious than sex. As a tween, your body is changing, your emotions are in flux, and you are likely to have a lot of questions. It's natural to want to find out more. Think about when you were a kid and where you tried to get answers about sex. Whether it was spying in your parents' closet or reading risqué magazines, today's children are a finger swipe on the iPad away from any sort of salacious information they desire. So what to do if you find your child has inadvertently—or not so inadvertently—come upon something? First, don't panic. This is not abnormal. This may be a good time to talk a little about what they are watching and what they think about it. You can then normalize the behavior and give them an example from your life when you did something similar as a pre-teen (or your brother/sister or a friend did something similar). It is normal for pre-teens to be curious and even potentially aroused by pornography. For example, data show that approximately 11 percent of boys age twelve and thirteen and 26 percent of boys age fourteen and fifteen report purposely viewing or downloading sexual images.[71]

Second, despite this being normal pre-teen and teenage behavior, you do also want to set limits. Online pornography, in general, is not appropriate for pre-teens and teenagers. Studies have found that teenagers who view pornography are more likely to view women as sexual playthings,[72] have more stereotyped gender attitudes,[73] display more sexually permissive behaviors, and are more likely to engage in sexual harassment in adolescence.[69,70] Thus, this is not something that pre-teens and teens should be allowed to view regularly, and safeguards and rules need to be

---

71 Wolak, J., K. Mitchell, and D. Finkelhor. 2007. Unwanted and wanted exposure to online pornography in a national sample of youth Internet users. *Pediatrics* 119(2): 247–57.

72 Peter, J., and P. M. Valkenburg. 2007. Adolescents' exposure to a sexualized media environment and their notions of women as sex objects. *Sex Roles* 56(5): 381–95.

73 Brown, J. D., K. L. L'Engle, 2009. X-rated: Sexual attitudes and behaviors associated with US early adolescents' exposure to sexually explicit media. *Communication Research* 36(1): 129–51.

put in place so that the pre-teen is not regularly accessing it. This can be done with some of the software discussed in Chapter 7.

Third, use this as an opportunity to engage with your child, provide correct information, or discuss your family's values. Talk about relationships and love and respect. Talk about how women are often portrayed in these types of videos and how this can have negative consequences for those who view it. You might even discuss how consent—two people wanting one another—is sexy. Remember that sexual curiosity is normal, but online pornography and its very mature themes should not be an acceptable route to satisfying that curiosity for a pre-teen.

What dangers should I warn my pre-teen about?

Remember that the danger of sexual abuse is seldom from strangers. Children at this stage will begin to spend more time alone with coaches, music teachers, caregivers, and the like. This is the stage at which sleepovers, whether at a friend's home, camp, or even a relative's house, begin to occur. The most important thing you can do is to speak openly with your child and provide a safe environment in which they can discuss their concerns. If you are uncomfortable talking about sex and shroud your language in secrecy, chances are your child will be uncomfortable talking about these things, too. While they should know not to allow a stranger to take them anywhere and that there are people in their community who can be trusted, we want to remind you that the best thing you can do is be connected to your tween and provide an environment in which they can open up and talk to you. Let your child know that if they feel uncomfortable in a situation, they should voice their concerns to someone or leave the situation. Let them know that you trust them, and encourage them to trust their own instincts as well.

We've recently heard about some parents who use the "x" system. Peer pressure is serious stuff whether you're twelve or twenty years old. If your child is in an uncomfortable situation, let them know that they can message you with a simple "x" and that you'll come get them, no questions asked. It simply gives them a safe out of whatever uncomfortable situation they are in and frees them of having to provide an explanation to their friends—or to you!

How much access should they have to social media at this point?

In addition to complying with age restrictions set up by social media sites themselves (see Chapter 7), we encourage you to set up your own rules and regulations. At this age, your tween's use of the Internet and social media sites should be monitored.

You may want to do the following:

1. Use safety software that bars access to inappropriate sites or prevents them from stumbling upon inappropriate sexual material.

2. Set rules and limits around their use. Decide on the number of hours per day and where in the house your child might access social media. For example, establish that Internet-enabled devices have to be used in common areas where you can monitor them.

3. Parent monitoring. At this age, safety and rule setting trumps privacy concerns. Set up the account with your child when you deem they are ready for it. Discuss cyberbullying, the exchange of sexual content, and what to do if someone they don't know tries to connect with them.

4. Educate yourself as much as possible. While most of us are familiar with "lol," "brb," and "omg," reading a tween's texts or chats will have you feeling like you have stumbled upon a new and very curious sounding language. Googling slang like "C9" (parent in room) or "RUH"

(are you horny?) can help you decipher what your pre-adolescent is talking about.

My child's friend sent him/her a nude or semi-nude photo. What should I do?

Tweens at this age tend to think of anything sex-related as silly. While photos that they share at this age are not likely to be overtly sexual, they may share photos that they have taken—such as a photo of a friend "mooning" someone. Or they may send one another something more sexually explicit. Use this as an opportunity to discuss what it means to share this kind of material and the ramifications of doing so. Open up the dialogue and ask them to consider the feelings of the person whose photo is being shared. What would it be like to be in their shoes? Ask them to think about how quickly a photo like that spreads: if the original sender sends it to just two people and every person thereafter sends it to just two people, by the end of the day their entire class or school may have seen it. This can result in embarrassment and depression. Once a nude photo is "out there," there is no way to get it back, and those kinds of photos can haunt individuals when they apply for college and jobs. What we most encourage you to do is to have your child practice critical thinking skills—to weigh the pros and cons of an action, to consider outcomes, and to assess the likelihood of those outcomes. These skills go far beyond that of the decision to send nude photos and will help your child develop the skills to navigate increasingly complex sexual and nonsexual situations in their life.

Most youth, and adults, don't think that sharing nude photos ("sexting") in this way qualifies as "child pornography," but when it involves the photo of a minor, it most certainly is. In some states, teens sending nude photos can be charged with felonies and have to register as a sex offender. Avoid lecturing, and, as noted above, put their critical thinking skills to work.

Ask your pre-teen to generate ideas about possible outcomes to sexting, which will help form the judgment and decision-making skills necessary to avoiding bad decisions.

My child is so independent now, should I be worried?

This is the age where we begin to leave them unsupervised with teachers, coaches, scout leaders, church mentors, or the parents of their friends. Children are perhaps the most vulnerable at this point as they begin to navigate the world alone, though they might still have very childlike understandings of the things around them. Above all, we encourage you to keep the lines of communication open. Giving them a regular time and place to talk to you will help them to open up. We know that most parents are strapped for time, and trips to the neighborhood café or long hikes in the woods may not be realistic week to week, but you can give your tween a special role in accompanying you to the grocery store each Saturday. This special and regular time together will also help you to be more observant of changes in behavior that are outside the realm of normal pre-teen stuff.

Take Home Message:

The pre-teen years are marked by a growing self-identity and independence. While still very much dependent upon parents, pre-teens are also at the start of puberty and may experience their first "puppy love." Their world is changing rapidly, and this is a key time to establish good and open communication. Most critical to this open communication is ensuring trust between you and your child. They should know that they can come to you with their concerns and that these concerns will be taken seriously. Having clear boundaries helps pre-teens navigate their increasingly complex world.

Box 12: Do You Know What Your Pre-Teens Are Doing?

A 2006 publication in the *American Journal of Family Therapy* explored the sex lives of pre-adolescent girls (between eight and thirteen years old) conversing in Internet chat rooms. The results presented a surprising, and somewhat concerning, portrait of pre-teen sexual awareness and sexual activity. Of the 1,300 girls who actively conversed, often explicitly, about sex online, approximately 30 percent were under twelve years old. Roughly 8 percent were younger than ten. Through online chats with these girls, researchers estimated that approximately 75 percent of the girls between thirteen and fifteen years old reported having engaged in sexual intercourse, while almost 50 percent of the girls between ten and thirteen said they had had sex.

Most concerning were data showing that up to 40 percent of girls who were under ten years old reported and described engaging in sexual activities. While these self-reports may not have been truthful or accurate, they nevertheless suggest that pre-teen and pre-adolescent girls may have a greater awareness of and possibly earlier experiences with sexual contact than is currently assumed. Although the researchers indicated that the highly sexualized experiences reported by these girls likely represented only a small percentage (roughly 1 percent) of the population of pre-teen girls, in the vast majority of these cases, the girls' parents were unaware of their sexual activity and sexual knowledge, and the girls themselves demonstrated a startling lack of awareness about the consequences of sexual behaviors, such as pregnancy, STDs, and psychological distress.

Atwood, J. D. 2006. Mommy's little angel, Daddy's little girl: Do you know what your pre-teens are doing? *The American Journal of Family Therapy* 34(5): 447–67.

CHAPTER 9

Talking to Your Teen

Being a parent of a teen can be challenging. With social pressures, academic expectations, and raging hormones, most parents report that the teenage years are harder than the toddler years (and we know those were tough!). Teenagers are going through a period of growth, both physically and emotionally. Their bodies are becoming sexually mature, and your son or daughter will start to look more like an adult than a child. Emotionally, they are trying to figure out who they are, and they seek independence from us. Naturally, this is a period of exploration as they try to navigate the world between childhood and adulthood, and inevitably, there will be some stumbles along the way. This is also a pivotal time for the formation of values and morals that will be ingrained in them for their adult life. Thus, it is very important that we as parents both teach and show them by example. In this chapter, we will talk about some of the challenges teenagers face. There continue to be dangers related to online solicitation, and as teens start to date and attend unsupervised parties, unwanted sexual contact should be a topic of conversation.

When do I start talking to my teen about dating violence?
Talking to children and teens about dating violence is hard but absolutely necessary. Many of us still have our romantic notions

of first love in its simplicity and innocence, and we hope this is the experience our children will have. The desire to not taint that romantic ideal is understandable. That being said, it is estimated that about one in three teenagers will be a victim of physical, sexual, emotional, or verbal abuse from a dating partner during adolescence.[74] One large study of teens aged between twelve and eighteen years found that 18 percent reported being sexually abused in their relationships.[75] Further, violence in relationships often starts between the ages of twelve and eighteen, which means that these are pivotal years to establish what are acceptable and unacceptable behaviors in a relationship. While these statistics encompass all types of violence, many are interrelated. Also, if children think that abuse—be it verbal, emotional, physical, or sexual—in a relationship is the norm, they may not seek more from future relationships. Teens should be taught that they are deserving of respect from their partners, that they ought to respect their partners, and that the presence of any form of abuse is unacceptable. Consequently, it is up to us as adults to provide them with guidance and to model these behaviors in our own lives.

Children are not taught how to behave in relationships in school. Children and teenagers learn from those around them, as well as from television and movies. Thus, you are probably the best role model they will have, and as a parent, you must take this role seriously. Parents must not only teach their children

---

74 Halpern, C. T., et al. 2001. Partner violence among adolescents in opposite-sex romantic relationships: Findings from the National Longitudinal Study of Adolescent Health. *American Journal of Public Health* 91(10): 1679-85.

75 Taylor, B. G. and E. A. Mumford. 2016. A national descriptive portrait of adolescent relationship abuse: Results from the National Survey on Teen Relationships and Intimate Violence. Journal of Interpersonal Violence 31(6): 963–88. doi: 10.1177/0886260514564070.

about how to treat others and how others should treat them but also model that behavior in our own relationships. For example, when you and your partner have an argument, your children will know whether you yell and scream at each other and call each other names or whether you discuss disagreements in a calm, collected way and come to an amicable decision. They will notice when you express physical affection for each other (and perhaps tell you it is gross). We not only have to talk the talk; we must also walk the walk. If you are a single parent, you can still model this behavior in your relationships with dating partners, friends, and family. The key is to instill a sense of worth in the teen and the expectation that they should be treated respectfully with kindness and love. The golden rule "do onto others as you would have them do onto you" is very applicable for teen relationships. Not only must they expect to be treated well, they must also understand that they, too, are responsible for respecting others and communicating effectively.

My teen isn't even dating yet—do we have to have that talk?
The short answer is yes: by the time your teen is dating, it may be too late to have the talk. Furthermore, as we have discussed in previous chapters, this should not be one talk but rather an ongoing conversation. See Box 14 for some examples for how to get conversations started.

Not only will you discuss the basics of the birds and the bees (a conversation that will start in childhood and evolve as your child gets older; see Box 7 for age-appropriate topics of conversation), but you will also talk about healthy relationships, effective communication, and personal safety.

It is important to let them know that it is normal to feel scared and uncomfortable about engaging in sexual behaviors—and that they do not have to do anything they are not ready to do. Let them know that someone who cares about them will respect that decision and will not push them to do anything they are not ready to do. This foundation will then stay with them as they journey through adolescence and into early adulthood.

This conversation will also depend upon your cultural beliefs about sexuality, which will affect how you talk to your children about sexual behavior and relationships. The biggest mistake, we believe, is doing nothing. While you may not condone premarital sexual behavior, your teenager might have different ideas. While this may not go along with your beliefs, punishing the behavior, pretending it is not happening, or avoiding the topic is not the way to go, either. It will only drive a wedge between you and your child and encourage them to keep secrets from you. Talk to your teen about your belief system and why you believe what you do. As you learned in Chapter 3, teens often share the values and beliefs of their family, so encouraging open and honest conversation increases the likelihood that they will behave in accordance with those family values.

I only have sons—what do I tell them?

Sexual violence prevention is not a topic to only talk to girls about. In fact, the most important conversations may be those we have with boys, as they are the perpetrators in many sexual assaults. One of the growing movements in sexual violence prevention is talking to and teaching boys, teenagers, and young men about respect, healthy relationships, and consent. While not all perpetrators of sexual violence are male, the majority are. Current theories suggest that these behaviors are learned and that they are based upon the way we socialize boys and men into their roles. For example, many consider sexually experienced male teenagers to be cool and manly, whereas sexually experienced teenage girls are thought to be "easy" or promiscuous. Data show that rigid gender role stereotypes—where men are expected to be more sexually aggressive and women more submissive—are related to increased levels of sexual violence.[76]

Despite these sociocultural factors that influence attitudes and beliefs, most boys and men will not engage in sexually violent behavior. However, we also want to teach them to step in whenever they encounter dangerous situations. For example, if their friends are speaking about girls in ways that are suggestive of sexual violence, they can let them know this is not cool. Further, if they see someone who is being victimized or just seems uncomfortable, they will know that they should intervene (even if just by stepping in to provide a distraction) or call for help.

Thus, it is important to teach your teenage sons about respect for women, and as much as possible, preach and model egalitarian values and beliefs. If you have both boys and girls, the research suggests that it is good to talk to them about these issues together so they can discuss each other's views and perspectives.

While the majority of teenage victims of sexual violence are girls, it's important to remember that boys can also be victimized. It is estimated that 18 percent of all victims of sexual assault under the age of eighteen are boys.[77] Boys may be especially vulnerable if they are gay (see next question) and exploring their sexual identity. We learned in Chapter 7 that online predators often solicit teenage boys in online forums.

My teen is non-gender conforming/LGBTQIA—do they face additional dangers?

The teenage years are hard for everyone, but LGTBQIA (Lesbian, Gay, Transgender, Bisexual, Queer, Intersex, and Asexual) and

---

76 Murnen, S. K., C. Wright, and G. Kaluzny. 2002. If "boys will be boys", then girls will be victims? *Sex Roles* 46(11-12): 359–75.

77 Department of Justice, Office of Justice Programs, Bureau of Justice Statistics, Sexual Assault of Young Children as Reported to Law Enforcement. 2000.

non-gender conforming youth may have particular challenges navigating adolescence, as they are not only discovering themselves but may also be subject to negative reactions and discrimination.

In addition, in a large multistate sample of LGB youth in grades nine through twelve, the CDC found that 18 to 29 percent reported dating violence in the past year and between 14 to 32 percent said that they were forced to have sexual intercourse against their will.[78] LGB youth are nearly twice as likely to be victims of sexual violence. Thus, if your teen identifies as LGBTQIA, you should talk to them about these risks and how to minimize the chances that they would be victimized. If they are being bullied at school, this behavior should immediately be reported to school authorities. Given that many LGBTQIA youth already feel isolated from peers and fear the admonishment of your family, it is even more important that you have open discussions and that their concerns are safe with you.

My teen has starting going to parties, and I suspect that there is drinking going on; how can I make sure they are safe?

Underage drinking is associated with many problems, one of which is increased risk of sexual assault. About one third of all rapes involve alcohol use by the perpetrator, the victim, or both.[79] It is important to have conversations with your teen about the dangers of underage drinking and what can happen.

Just because there is drinking going on, though, doesn't mean that you should assume necessarily that your teen is participating

---

78 Centers for Disease Control and Prevention. Sexual identity, sex of sexual contacts, and health-risk behaviors among students in grades 9–12—Youth Risk Behavior Surveillance, selected sites, United States, 2001–2009. *MMWR*. 2011.

79 Miller, J. W., T. S. Naimi, R. D. Brewer, and S. E. Jones. 2007. Binge drinking and associated health risk behaviors among high school students. *Pediatrics* 119(1): 76–85.

or knew about it ahead of time. Situations can often change very quickly. As part of having open communication about these issues, you should have some sort of agreement with your teen that they can call you if they ever feel unsafe or uncomfortable without feeling that they will be subject to a lecture or punishment. While a "debrief" may be warranted the next day, stay away from the "I told you so's" and removal of privileges, as that will only decrease the likelihood that your teen will reach out for help the next time. If there is another teenager or young adult in the family who has a driver's license, they should also be made available to be contacted should the need arise. Teenagers often feel more comfortable reaching out to their siblings or cousins, for example, rather than a parent. The important thing to remember is that they have made a good decision by asking for help when they needed it and that should be reinforced and supported, not punished.

We have already talked about online safety—what else do we have to know?

As discussed in Chapter 8, sexting is something that should be on your radar. Research has shown that many teens and young adults share nude or semi-nude pictures with one another as a technological means of flirting or showing interest (courtship behaviors).[80] While teens may believe this to be harmless, these types of images can be quickly disseminated to large numbers of people. While some apps, such as Snapchat, allow photos to disappear after they are viewed, people can take screenshots of the images and forward them. Your teen needs to learn that anything that is sent via text or e-mail can be forwarded and placed on the

---

80 Kaylor, L., E. L. Jeglic, and C. Collins. 2016. Examining the impact of technology on exhibitionistic behavior. *Deviant Behavior* 37(10): 1152–1162. doi.org/10.1080/01639625.2016.1169828.

Internet permanently for all to see. This has led to consequences such as depression, harassment, and in some cases even suicide.[81]

In addition, having or forwarding/sending nude or seminude photos of those who are underage can result in sex crime charges for possessing or transmitting child pornography. While the majority of cases that are prosecuted involve an adult as well as a teen, about 18 percent of the cases in which charges were pressed involved teens who were only "experimenting," and in a couple of extreme cases these teens even ended up on a sex offender registry.[82] Thus, it is imperative to impart upon your teen that under no circumstance should they take or send nude or seminude pictures of themselves or others, period.

Finally, as we learned in Chapter 7, some teens may talk to strangers online through chat rooms or on their smartphones. In some cases, this talk might become sexualized, and teens who are vulnerable or who recently experienced a loss may be particularly susceptible to entering into relationships with strangers online. Thus, general parental oversight and monitoring of what teens are doing online or with their apps is warranted.

I found out that my teen has been deleting messages he/she doesn't want me to see—what should I do?

While this is potentially disconcerting, it is normal teenage behavior. Did we want our parents listening in our own phone calls when we were teenagers? Of course not; and similarly they do not want us to know everything they are doing or saying, either. Just as a diary should afford a teen a private place to express their

---

81 Meyer, E. J. (December 16, 2009). 'Sexting' and suicide. *Psychology Today.* Retrieved from https://www.psychologytoday.com/blog/gender-and-schooling/200912/sexting-and-suicide.

82 Wolak, J., D. Finkelhor, K. J. Mitchell. 2012. How often are teens arrested for sexting? Data from a national sample of police cases. *Pediatrics* 129(1): 4–12.

feelings, a teen should also be afforded some degree of privacy on their phone, as well.

This, however, does come with a caveat. In Chapter 7, we discussed ways to monitor kids online without invading their privacy or overwhelming them with your presence, one of which was talking to your children about having access to their online usernames and passwords. Then, if there is cause for concern—for example, you know that your teen is lying to you or there is a sudden change in their behavior—you have the resources you need to check up on your teen according to the limitations or contract set up when the child/teen received their phone. You should always have their passwords for online accounts, smartphones, iPad, etc., and while the general agreement is that you will not be spying on them, you have already set up the right to check what they are doing periodically. This is especially true if you suspect there is something going on that they are not sharing with you.

Your first course of action should always be to try and talk to them; however, if they are not sharing with you and you are worried, you can go back to the contract that was set up.

While it is important to be able to access their online accounts, you do not want to violate your agreement with them unless you feel like they are in danger or engaging in risky behavior. Just as you want them to trust you, you also have to trust them. Teens that we have spoken to have told us that once that trust is lost, they experience less guilt about going behind their parents' backs.

Some of my daughter's/son's friends are dating adults—how do I handle this?

To teenagers, dating an "older man" or "older woman" seems like the epitome of cool. However, as adults we know that there is something wrong with an adult man wanting to date a teenage girl or an adult woman wanting to date a teenage boy.

Depending upon your location, the age of the teen, and the age difference between the teen and the adult, if sexual relations take place, this is considered statutory rape. Statutory rape refers to sexual behavior where one of the individuals is unable to consent, due to their age. For example, even if a thirteen-year-old willingly agrees to or even initiates sex, under the law they are considered unable to consent because of their age. This is a sex crime, and the adult can face a lengthy prison sentence and years on the sex offender registry.

I saw that my teens' friends are sending them racy and sexual pictures via Snapchat and text—what should I do?

As mentioned above, have a talk with your teen about the consequences of having these types of images on social media. Not only is it a possible sex crime, but these images can also be forwarded to the whole school or posted online, where they might rapidly reach a very wide audience. These images do not go away and can impact their future schooling and employment prospects as many colleges and employers now Google potential applicants. As educators, we have not interviewed students for our doctoral program when we saw inappropriate material posted on their Facebook page. This should be a community effort—if you know the parents of your child's friends, for example, you should alert them to what their teen is doing in the event that they are not aware.

My teenagers say they feel like I am spying on them when I check their social media and texts—how do I handle this?

The use of social media is a privilege, not a right. As noted before, the rules for social media and smartphone use need to be established when your child first begins using these platforms and devices. As your teen gets older, you will want to give them more privacy, and you can renegotiate the terms of when you will and will not monitor their online behaviors. However, you are ultimately responsible for their welfare, and you have to let them know that if they are not sharing information with you and their behavior is concerning (change in mood, lying, sneaking out), then you will have to check on what is going on so you can help them and make sure they are safe.

Take Home Message:
The teenage years can be tumultuous for even the most seasoned parent. Not only is your teen figuring out who they are, but they are also beginning to enter into romantic relationships and attend unsupervised parties. These are new experiences, ones that pose potential dangers for teens. While their bodies are starting to resemble those of adults, their brains are still not fully developed and their thinking is, in many ways, still quite childlike. Thus, it is imperative that we as parents provide guidance as they navigate these new unchartered waters. Though we want to provide them with increased independence, we still need to know what they are doing and with whom they are doing it. Keeping the lines of communication open can be more challenging during this period of development, but if you have already set the stage for open communication, most teens will continue to talk to you. Additionally, you can teach them by modeling appropriate behavior—your teens are watching how you navigate conflicts and how you behave in relationships; thus it is important that you lead by example.

**Box 13: Talking to Your Teen
about Dating Violence is Hard**

Below are some websites with specific strategies, tips, and programs that could be helpful.

Futures without Violence: https://www.futureswithoutviolence .org/talk-teens-teen-dating-violence/

Break the Cycle: Breakthecycle.org

US Department of Health and Human Services: https://www.acf .hhs.gov/blog/2017/02/can-you-talk-to-teens-about-healthy-relationships-and-teen-dating-violence

Dating Matters Program: https://vetoviolence.cdc.gov/dating -matters

---

Box 14: Sample Conversation Starters with Teens

Many of these conversations are easier to have informally when your kids are not looking directly at you. For example, times when you are driving them back and forth to activities are great opportunities to bring up these issues informally. Below are some suggestions for conversation starters.

1. "Did you see what is going on with <insert current event that involves sexual abuse>. What do you think about that?"
2. "Have you had any more talks in health class about sex and consent? What kinds of things are they talking to you about?"
3. "I saw some really inappropriate posts the other day from X's daughter on Facebook; do any of your friends do things like that on social media? What do you think the consequences may be?"
4. "I heard that X and Y are dating; how is their relationship? How do they treat one another?"

CHAPTER 10

The College Years—with Great Freedom Comes Great Responsibility

If you are like us, you have probably at some point looked back on your college years and said to yourself, "What was I thinking?" From where we sit now—in homes filled with sippy cups and talk of college savings plans—the debauchery-filled years of college bring lots of memories. But for some, those memories are not all positive. National data show that over a quarter (27.5 percent) of women are sexually assaulted during their college years and 7.7 percent of college-aged men report engaging in behavior that meets the legal definition of rape.[83] However not all unwanted sexual behavior is what we think of as traditional rape. About 44 percent of college women and 19 percent of college men report having been coerced into sexual behavior—this means that they are pressured or forced either verbally or physically to engage in

---

83 Koss, M. P., C. A. Gidycz, and N. Wisniewski. 1987. The scope of rape: Incidence and prevalence of sexual aggression and victimization in a national sample of higher education students. *Journal of Consulting and Clinical Psychology 55(2): 162–170.*

sexual behavior that they do not want to do. Sexual assault and sexual coercion can affect mental health, physical health, social relationships, college GPA, and overall academic success.

Whether your child will live on or near campus or live at home, college is a time of great freedom and newfound independence. New friends. New experiences. And, of course, new dangers. In this chapter, we aim to guide you as a parent to help your child make responsible decisions as they embark upon this new phase in their lives.

What should I talk to my son about as he heads off to college?

Talk to my son? you might be thinking. *But he's 6'2" and hardly needs my protection anymore.* It is emblematic of our cultural view on sex and sexual violence that we tell women what to do—or *not* do—to protect themselves, but we don't have as much to say to young men. As we began to discuss in Chapter 9, ensuring that your son doesn't engage in coercive sexual behavior is as, if not more, important as ensuring that your daughter is kept safe. In fact, we consider these conversations that you have with young men to be critical to the prevention of sexual violence. While these conversations were started in their teenage years, in many cases your young adults are now living on their own with newfound independence.

Keep in mind, however, that your son could be the perpetrator of a sexual assault just as he could be a victim of or witness to a sexual assault. Some 8 percent of college-aged men report being sexually victimized,[84] and many more are bystanders each year to risky peer behavior, where they have the opportunity to

---

84   Barnyard, V. L., S. Ward, E. S. Cohn, C. Moorhead, and W. Walsh. 2007. Unwanted sexual contact on campus: A comparison of women's and men's experiences. *Violence and Victims* 22(1): 52–70.

intervene in some way to potentially prevent someone from being victimized.

These conversations will hopefully occur amidst a backdrop of your family showing respect for others. As we started to talk about in Chapter 9, men who grow up watching their parents treat one another with respect and who appreciate and acknowledge the rights and dignity of others—whether they be cashiers or taxi drivers or colleagues—will be more likely to model that behavior. Furthermore, we are now teaching them to become adults themselves, and you are the adult that they are most likely to emulate. Thus the guidance you give them will be most effective if you have modeled this type of behavior in your own relationships and interactions. If you haven't always modeled that behavior, acknowledge your mistakes and start now. We often teach our children the most valuable life lessons when we recognize our own failings and acknowledge how we have learned from them. Recently, a friend of ours was coaching a little league baseball game with his young sons. He told us that he lost his cool with a young umpire and was later berated by the parents watching the game. What stood out to us—and very likely made an impression on his sons too—was not the mistake he made, but how he handled it. He acknowledged his behavior openly, saying that it reminded him that "we're all out there doing our best and nobody's perfect" and vowed to do better next time. Making mistakes is part of life. You will no doubt lose your cool in front of your children or display imperfect behavior from time to time. But how we handle these mistakes and show respect to others will serve as an important guide they can follow.

Talking to young men about consent cannot be underestimated. The pain and suffering of a victim is, of course, the most obvious concern. But perpetrators of sexual assaults also can end up on a sex offender registry, which, as discussed in Chapter 2, brings with it a host of sometimes lifelong negative consequences, such as difficulty finding employment or housing that comes with being marked as an offender. So remind your son of the importance of respecting the rights of others, but also discuss the impact that this could have on his own life.

People who are sleeping or drunk or semi-conscious cannot give consent. And you cannot assume that silence equals consent. Consent can, of course, change through the course of a sexual experience. Someone may start out by saying yes to certain sexual acts, but then change their mind to no. Consent is not a moment-in-time thing that you check off, but more of a continuing conversation. If in doubt, ask. And even if not in doubt, still ask. Some states now require affirmative consent.

This all sounds so simple, but my son's brain often takes a backseat to his hormones.

First, rest assured that your son is not alone. Sexual urges can be powerful in adolescence and early adulthood. But the adolescent brain—still in development until the early twenties—is best considered a work in progress. The prefrontal cortex, which moderates judgment, risk-taking, and impulsivity, is among the last areas of the brain to fully develop. Because of this, college students likely cannot fully appreciate the risks of a situation as we do. Their risk perception, or ability to make decisions about how dangerous behavior is—whether their own or that of others—is underdeveloped. Data show that adolescent boys have empathy deficits, meaning that it will be more difficult for them to take the perspective of others. What can you do to facilitate cerebral connections? Simply telling your child to do or not do something doesn't get the gears of their brain working. Instead, encourage critical thought. Open up discussions where you get them to discuss how alcohol affects the brain. Learn the facts yourselves so that you can guide the discussion, but let them draw out the conclusions. With regard to empathy, ask them to put themselves in the position of others. From even a very young age, you should encourage them to consider what another person may be thinking or feeling.

Box 15: The Consequences of Excessive Drinking

Most people are familiar with the hangover—the almost unavoidable consequence of a night of drinking alcohol. However, research shows that excessive alcohol consumption can have a range of more severe and debilitating consequences that can't be resolved with some Gatorade and a big breakfast. The risk of consequences is particularly high, with national estimates reporting increased instances of death, injury, physical assault, sexual assault, unsafe sex, health problems, suicide attempts, drunk driving, memory loss, police involvement, and alcohol dependence among college students who drink versus students who don't drink. In a study of eight hundred college students, 51 percent reported that they had experienced at least one alcohol blackout in their lives. Such blackouts can lead to even more dangerous consequences, like sexual assault or potentially fatal alcohol toxicity. Acute alcohol toxicity, which occurs when the effects of alcohol suppress the brain stem and depress breathing, accounted for thirty thousand hospitalizations nationwide for eighteen to twenty-four years over a ten-year period.

Excessive or binge drinking can also affect academic performance. About 25 percent of college students have reported that their drinking habits cause their academic performance to deteriorate, and survey studies suggest that college students who binge drink are almost six times more likely to perform poorly on a test, five times more likely to miss class, and four times more likely to report memory loss. Other studies have indicated possible associations between binge drinking and college dropout rates, as well as links between excessive drinking in college and alcohol dependence later in life.

White, A. and R. Hingson. 2014. The burden of alcohol use: Excessive alcohol consumption and related consequences among college students. *Alcohol Research* 35(2): 201–218.

What should I talk to my daughter about as she heads off to college?

The risk to women probably seems more obvious: campus parties, "roofies," jungle juice spiked with high alcohol content liquor, STDs and STIs, and date rape. As noted earlier, close to half (44 percent) of college-aged women report having been sexually coerced in some manner. Young women are especially at risk when they first start college. Students are often informed on college campuses of a high risk "red zone," often defined as the period between the start of school in late August and the Thanksgiving Day break in November. Data show that freshmen are more at risk of unwanted sexual experiences than are older students and that this risk is indeed especially high for students during the first few months of their first year (i.e., during the red zone).[85] This is often the first time they are away from home for a prolonged period, and they have more freedoms and easier access to things that may impair judgment, such as alcohol and drugs.

Data also show that young women underestimate personal risk. In a classic "this won't happen to me" kind of way, research shows that women have an *optimistic bias* that lends them to think that their chance of experiencing sexual assault is less than that of their peers and, moreover, that they are better able to handle high risk situations than are others.[86] With this in mind, consider the importance of discussing sexual assault as something that can happen to someone like you or even *you*! These discussions should also address their ability to manage risk. It's better

85 Kimble, M., A. D. Neacsiu, W. F. Flack, and W. F. Horner. 2008. Risk of unwanted sex for college women: Evidence for a red zone. *Journal of American College Health* 57(3): 331–37.

86 Untied, A. S. and C. L. Dulaney. 2015. College students' perceived risk of sexual victimization and the role of optimistic bias. *Journal of Interpersonal Violence* 30(8): 1417–31.

not to test how well one manages a difficult situation when you know that, for many victims, these situations have pernicious consequences.

However, before you encourage your daughter to take a class in self-defense, to avoid frat parties, to avoid walking alone at night, and to limit drinking, we ask that you pause to consider how we as a society put the responsibility for sexual assaults on young women. We're not saying, for example, that being careful not to leave your drink unattended or to walk alone are not wise decisions (as they probably are); rather, we are saying to consider how we as a society have historically made preventing sexual assaults to be the work of women. We do encourage you to have conversations in which you encourage your daughter to trust her gut, to extricate herself from situations that feel uncomfortable in some way, to develop safe habits, and to consider the outcomes of actions. But we hope that you will exercise caution and consider the way you frame these discussions, as the way we have traditionally framed this contributes to the guilt, shame, and responsibility that victims often feel after an assault (see Box 16). As with conversations with young men, stern lectures are best avoided while discussions that encourage critical thinking and help to sharpen risk perception skills are most likely to be helpful. Finally, a reminder that encourages safety, but serves to remind that women are not to blame for the assaultive actions of others, can go a long way in building self-confidence around issues of personal safety.

Box 16: Victim Blaming

How old are you? How much do you weigh? What did you eat that day? Well, what did you have for dinner? Who made dinner? Did you drink with dinner? No, not even water? When did you drink? How much did you drink? What container did you drink out of? Who gave you the drink? How much do you usually drink? Who dropped you off at this party? At what time? But where exactly? What were you wearing? Why were you going to this party? What did you do when you got there? Are you sure you did that? But what time did you do that? What does this text mean? Who were you texting? When did you urinate? Where did you urinate? With whom did you urinate outside? Was your phone on silent when your sister called? Do you remember silencing it? Really, because on page 53, I'd like to point out that you said it was set to ring. Did you drink in college? You said you were a party animal? How many times did you black out? Did you party at frats? Are you serious with your boyfriend? Are you sexually active with him? When did you start dating? Would you ever cheat? Do you have a history of cheating? What do you mean when you said you wanted to reward him? Do you remember what time you woke up? Were you wearing your cardigan? What color was your cardigan? Do you remember any more from that night? No? Okay, well, we'll let Brock fill it in.

I was pummeled with narrowed, pointed questions that dissected my personal life, love life, past life, family life; inane questions, accumulating trivial details to try and find an excuse for this guy who had me half naked before even bothering to ask for my name. After a physical assault, I was assaulted with questions designed to attack me, to say, "See, her facts don't line up, she's out of her mind, she's practically an alcoholic, she probably wanted to hook up, he's like an athlete, right, they were both drunk, whatever, the hospital stuff she remembers is after the fact, why take it into account, Brock has a lot at stake so he's having a really hard time right now."

Excerpt from victim impact statement in People v. Turner. 2015. Full Letter: www.paloaltoonline.com/news/2016/06/03/stanford-sex-assault-victim-you-took-away-my-worth

Last but not least, ensure that your daughter is aware of crime reporting procedures and how to contact the campus safety office. Make sure she knows that if she is ever victimized, she can reach out to you, another family member, a friend, or someone at her college and university and that she should not be afraid to ask for help. Most sexual assault victims never report their crimes, often because they don't think they will be believed, because they feel shame about the experience, or because they don't consider something like a date rape to be a "real" sexual assault. If in doubt, victims should disclose and report.

Are men always the aggressors and women always the victims?

Of course not. By now, one thing that has hopefully been clear from this book is that sexual assaults often don't fit the stereotype, and this is true in the case of campus sexual assault. Women engage in sexually coercive behavior against men, and sexual assaults occur in same sex encounters, i.e., men perpetrate offenses against other men just as women perpetrate offenses against other women. In fact, sexual-minority students are at especially high risk of sexual violence. Data show that male and female sexual-minority students' experience about double the rate of victimization than do heterosexual students.[87]

What can I do to protect my child?

While concerns about your child's safety may have you dreading the day they walk out the door to start college, we have to respect their independence and recognize that this is a natural

---

87 K. M., et al. 2015. Physical dating violence, sexual violence, and unwanted pursuit victimization: A comparison of incidence rates among sexual-minority and heterosexual college students. *Journal of Interpersonal Violence* 30(4): 580-600. doi: 10.1177/0886260514535260.

part of their growth into adulthood. Rather than constantly telling them what to do and not to do (as we did when they were little), you should remind them that you are an ally. When we talked to groups of our college-aged students, one thing we commonly heard was that they liked hearing from their parents that they could contact them via text or phone if they were in trouble, that their parents would be there for them, and that there would be no questions asked.

While not all youth live close enough to home during college that their parents can come and get them, this kind of support is still welcome. While most of the young adults we talked to never took their parents up on the offer, it still meant something to them. And some did take their parents up on the offer. One thing was clear, however: students don't want to be lectured for getting themselves into some kind of bad situation. So if you say that your child can contact you when they are in trouble, no questions asked—you have to mean it. This doesn't mean that you ignore it and not say anything at all. A debriefing, with emphasis on the "brief," is important here.

While it's important to talk about risk, it's also important to talk about how to manage that risk. Avoid exaggerating the risk and simply elevating fear. Instead, provide them with actual data and work with them to process solutions that can keep them safe. It's not going to be very useful, for example, to tell your child to never have a drink, but you can process with them how judgment is impaired when we drink and how impaired judgment could affect them in various types of situations, whether with friends, in an automobile, or out at a bar.

Box 17: Facts about Campus Sexual Violence

Over the past decade, awareness of sexual violence occurring on college campuses has drastically increased. But what are the facts about campus sexual violence? A study by the US Department of Justice found that rates of rape and sexual assault were highest among college-aged females as compared to females in other age groups. In about 80 percent of cases, the victim knew the offender, and perhaps because of this familiarity, female students were less likely than nonstudents to report the assault to the police. Furthermore, only 16 percent of female students who were sexually victimized received some kind of assistance from a victim services agency.

Students were more likely to be victimized by a friend or an acquaintance, as opposed to an intimate partner or stranger, and in 47 percent of cases examined, the offender was believed to be under the influence or alcohol or drugs. Use of a weapon was reported in about 11 percent of cases, and the majority of reported assaults occurred away from the victim's home or dormitory.

Sinozich, S. and L. Langton. 2014. Rape and sexual assault victimization among college-aged females, 1995–2013. *US Department of Justice, Bureau of Justice Statistics: Special Report.*

What about sororities and fraternities?

There are many positives associated with sororities and fraternities. College students have the opportunity to be part of something, and these social connections and support can be especially helpful as they navigate alone in a new world far from the comforts of home, old friends, and old ways. However, while there are many positives associated with sororities and fraternities, when it comes to sexual assault it's important to know that membership is associated with increased risk.[85, 86]

Important socialization takes place in sororities and fraternities. Certain behaviors and attitudes are reinforced and rewarded. Male peer groups may reward hyper-masculine behavior, the objectification of women, excessive alcohol consumption—all things known to predict sexual assaults. As they face new college experiences, males in fraternities and on athletic teams will turn to their peer groups for support. Sexual assaults more often occur in these settings that enforce a rigid gender ideology and enforce peer pressure for sex. Alcohol consumption, associated with membership in fraternities, also predicts perpetration of sexual offenses.[88] For these reasons, data also show that certain groups of college-aged men—including fraternity members and members of athletic teams—are at increased risk for the perpetration of sexual assault.

Sorority group membership is also a risk factor, which may relate to increased rates of alcohol consumption, adherence to rigid gender ideologies, and value placed on physical attractiveness and an especially feminine lifestyle.[89] Additionally, female sororities increase access to environments (e.g., frat parties) that provide opportunities for perpetrators to come into contact with vulnerable women.

So, while fraternities and sororities are not all bad, they are associated with circumstances and behaviors—as well as ideologies—that increase the risk sexual assault. If your child decides to join a fraternity or a sorority, it's important that you discuss the risks with them.

My daughter is safe because she is in a relationship, right?

Hookups in college—or casual sex with someone you are not dating—are common, with some 40 percent of female college students hooking up with someone during their first year of

88 National Institute of Justice. 2008. Factors that increase sexual assault risk. Retrieved from https://www.nij.gov/topics/crime/rape-sexual-violence/campus/Pages/increased-risk.aspx.

89 Franklin, C. A. 2016. Sorority affiliation and sexual assault victimization: Assessing vulnerability using path analysis. *Violence Against Women* 22(8): 895–922.

college.[90] What's much more common is sex within a relationship, with some 56 percent of first year female college students engaging in sexual relations with a romantic partner.[90] But sexual assaults and coercive sexual behavior on campus also happen frequently in the context of relationships (and are perpetrated by people whom many consider to be "nice guys"), so be careful not to make the assumption that being in a relationship negates risk. One study found that 24 percent of college students who were sexually assaulted reported that the perpetrator was a current or former intimate partner.[91]

Are some colleges safer than others?

The Clery Act[92] (named for Jeanne Clery) requires colleges to track and report sexual assaults and other crime statistics to inform students and their families about the safety of campuses. And with growing awareness of the problem of campus sexual assault and its many consequences, there have been increased calls—from the National Institute of Justice, from the White House Task Force to Protect Students from Sexual Assaults, and from the American College Health Association—to prevent and respond to the problem of sexual violence. Part of this is reporting rates of sexual violence.

When deciding where to send your child to college, look up the college's website to see whether their policy on sex crimes is clearly stated and find data on how often assaults have been reported. Keep in mind, however, that a listing of sexual assaults

90   Fielder, R. L., K. B. Carey, and M. P. Carey. 2013. Are hookups replacing romantic relationships? A longitudinal study of first-year female college students. *Journal of Adolescent Health* 52(5): 657–59.

91   Sinozich, S. and L. Langton. 2014. Rape and sexual assault victimization among college-aged females, 1995–2013. *US Department of Justice, Bureau of Justice Statistics: Special Report.*

92   20 USC. § 1092(f) (2012).

in not necessarily a bad thing as it may be indicative of open and clear reporting policies and a campus environment that takes assaults seriously.

What does it mean that my child's college has an affirmative consent policy?

Many of us grew up hearing "no means no," meant to signal that when someone says "no" to sexual activities, that "no" should be respected. California was the first state to establish a "yes means yes" standard. For consent to be obtained, "yes means yes" means that a partner has to affirmatively agree to sexual relations. It is not enough to simply intuit that one wants to engage in sexual relations. The University of California's policy, for example, considers consent to be an "affirmative, unambiguous, and conscious decision by each participant to engage in mutually agreed upon sexual activity."[93] In 2015, New York State also signed into law an affirmative consent policy, and certain universities (e.g., University of Minnesota; Texas A&M; University of Virginia; Indiana University; Stanford University; Yale University; University of New Hampshire; University of Illinois, Urbana-Champaign)[94] require affirmative consent as well. Whether or not you are in California or New York or at a university that uses an affirmative consent standard, it's more than a good idea to ensure that your partner is willing. It is also recommended that consent is reaffirmed throughout the sexual encounter as consent can change over time. For example, a partner may be okay with kissing and fondling but may not feel comfortable engaging in intercourse. In other words, consent for one act should not be assumed just because consent for a different act was given.

---

93 University of California Policy, *Sexual Harassment and Sexual Violence*: http://policy.ucop.edu/doc/4000385/SHSV.

94 See www.endrapeoncampus.org.

They're adults now, so isn't my job done?

No. Most kids get some kind of education about campus sexual assault at college orientation. But don't leave this job to anyone else. This information will be best received when it is part of a continuing conversation, one that you have been having since your son or daughter was in kindergarten. Though some of you might balk at the notion of repeated conversations about sex, the good news is that issues like consent and drinking and respect for bodily autonomy can happen in a million different ways throughout the course of childhood.

Take Home Message:

Continuing to have open discussions with your children—both sons and daughters—is especially important as they head off to college. The first semester of college is an especially high-risk period for young women. Conversations should also be had with young men, because they are most often the perpetrators of campus sexual assaults, and also because they can be victimized, too. Make yourself aware of your child's college's rules around consent so you can talk to your son or daughter about this. Should the unthinkable occur, you also want to be sure that you can provide them with resources on where they can go to report a crime and get help in their local community.

CHAPTER 11

What to Do If You Suspect a Child Has Been Abused

So far we've been discussing ways to keep children safe, in the hopes of preventing abuse or assaults from happening in the first place. But now we want to shift focus and provide details on what to do if you suspect a child is already being sexually abused. Remember that most children *don't* report their abuse. Studies show that only around a third of victims disclose their abuse during childhood.[95] The majority of childhood abuse victims wait until adulthood to disclose abuse, if they disclose it at all. Therefore, it is especially important that we remain vigilant to the possibility of abuse in our communities. Intervening can prevent the continuation of abuse or prevent another person becoming victimized.

Throughout much of this book, we've tried to urge you to relax your fears and allow your children to play in parks and be provided with age-appropriate independence. As we have discussed, the risk of a sex crime happening in a stereotypical

---

95 London, K., M. Bruck, S. Ceci, and D. W. Shuman. 2005. Disclosure of child sexual abuse: What does the research tell us about the ways that children tell? *Psychology, Public Policy, and Law* 11(1): 194–226.

"stranger danger" situation is much lower than most people assume. So, while we encourage you to relieve yourself of worry over statistically improbable events, we'd also like to ask you to be more vigilant about things that happen right underneath your nose. A child in your vicinity could be suffering abuse. With one in six boys and one in four girls being sexually abused before the age of eighteen,[96] it's not implausible that a child you know could be suffering sexual abuse.

Whether or not you know a child in this situation, it's quite likely that you have been exposed to attitudes supportive of sexual violence in your lifetime. While that notion might not immediately ring true for you, remember that attitudes and cultural norms are often so ingrained that we barely notice them. When you hear of a college woman who was sexually assaulted at a party, is your first thought to wonder if she is telling the truth? Do you wonder why she was alone in a bar or question how much she drank? Do you think men should be the initiators of sex and be ready for sex all the time? These are all the sorts of attitudes that help nurture a culture of sexual assault and abuse. Being vigilant about sexual violence under our noses can include proactive efforts to help a child, intervening in a situation where someone is at risk, or simply working to help change cultural attitudes supportive of sexual violence.

In this chapter, we provide data that will help guide your response if you think a child is in danger. We also encourage you to take action as a community member and potential bystander by examining your own thinking, challenging the thinking of others, and intervening if a situation seems like it could turn dangerous.

---

96 Centers for Disease Control and Prevention. 2005. Adverse childhood experiences study: Data and statistics. Atlanta, GA: Centers for Disease Control and Prevention, National Center for Injury Prevention and Control. Retrieved from http://www.cdc.gov/violenceprevention/acestudy/index.html.

What kind of signs might indicate that a child is being sexually abused?

Physical signs are not always obvious. For example, a child who is being abused will not likely have bruises, cuts, or scratches. Instead, you may notice behavioral indicators from the child or the perpetrator. Though it was once believed that sexually abused children exhibited a specific "syndrome" of symptoms, we now know that symptoms of abuse don't always fit a clear pattern. In fact, some children who are abused show no symptoms or behavioral changes at all. Others may act withdrawn, isolated, or fearful. Self-blame and shame are common, as abuse is often shrouded in secrecy. Some children may show age-inappropriate sexual knowledge or imitate sexual acts. While developmentally appropriate sexual exploration is normal among children of all ages, overly sexualized behavior in young children or especially promiscuous ways of acting among older children can be red flags.[97] While any one of these behavioral signs are seldom a tell-tale marker for sexual abuse, a pattern of signs—including any kind of behavior that is outside the norm for the child—is worth paying attention to.

Additionally, you might notice odd behaviors on the part of the alleged perpetrator, such as going to great efforts to be alone with the child or having a special relationship that involves lots of individualized attention or special gifts. Secret keeping is also a red flag. Though innocent little secrets may not, at first, seem too worrisome, remember that perpetrators sometimes want to feel out their victims and set the stage for bigger secrets later on. Some perpetrators might try to desensitize a child to physical touch through tickling, wrestling, or other hands-on physical activities.

---

97 Finkelhor, D. 1984. *Child Sexual Abuse: New Theory and Research*. New York: Free Press, 1984.

The dynamic between the child and perpetrator should also be observed. If a child acts funny around or seems to want to avoid a certain person, pay attention to this. They may not be able to verbalize this, but a gut feeling should not be ignored. Moreover, if the dynamic causes you to raise eyebrows, it's wise to avoid leaving a child alone with this person. If you think there is cause for concern, you might also talk to others—such as a schoolteacher or soccer coach—to see if they've noticed anything unusual. Getting someone else's perspective can help confirm or disconfirm your concerns. You want to be careful not to sully the reputation of someone, so exercise caution here, but if it is a real concern remember that the safety of a child is more important than protecting the feelings of someone else.

Most importantly, we suggest you talk to the child. Open up a dialogue, and give them the opportunity to talk. Children in these situations may not have anyone to talk to, may not think they will be believed, or may not even know that what is happening to them is abusive. However, you want to be careful, especially with very young children, to not use suggestive words and phrases that plant ideas in their mind. Instead, use open-ended questions and allow the child to use his or her own words to describe what—if anything—went on.

This is such a hard topic; I'm not sure what to even say to a child in this situation.

Whether you suspect abuse or a child has spontaneously reported abuse to you, the most important thing is to stay calm and keep your own emotions in check. You may feel like crying or you may be so angry that you want to scream, but what the child needs is somebody who provides a safe and supportive space for them to talk about what is going on.

This may not happen overnight, so be careful not to rush things. A child who has been threatened in some way or who has been groomed to trust the perpetrator is not likely to reveal what's going on the first time he or she is asked. Give a child space and time to disclose; he or she may be putting out their own feelers to ensure that disclosure will not cause more suffering for them. A child may also be scared to tell as the perpetrator has told them that they or their loved ones may be harmed if they talk about what is going on.

If a child has disclosed abuse to you, the most important thing is to simply listen. Give them space to talk without pressuring them for details. Let them know they did the right thing in deciding to talk to you and tell them that you believe them, will help them, and will keep them safe. Self-blame is such a big part of this, and a child needs to know that it's not their fault. You may experience self-blame also or not be sure how to handle the emotions that emerge. Just as we encourage a child to seek help from a competent and understanding adult, we also encourage you to seek help from a friend, spouse, or trusted acquaintance who is knowledgeable and supportive and who will help guide you through this difficult time.

What if the child or adolescent doesn't know that it is abuse?

It's worth noting that a child may not recognize what is happening as abuse. Younger children may not yet fully understand what sexual behavior is, while older youth may understand but consider it to be consensual. Abusers are notorious for using manipulative tactics that lead a child to blame themselves or question the authenticity of what is going on. Moreover, abuse can be especially difficult to understand if the perpetrator is someone you like, respect, or consider yourself to be in a relationship with— and most perpetrators fall into these categories. Some youth have a sexual response (e.g., erection or orgasm) to abuse. Though this is the body's normal reaction to sexual stimulation, it can be part of what makes it difficult to understand the behavior as being abusive.

It's not unusual for children to blame themselves, whether because of a sexual response, because of their special relationship with the perpetrator, or because they think there is something they did to have caused this. For these reasons and many others, a child who is being abused may have a clouded understanding of the situation.

Should I let the child know if I plan to report the abuse?

Yes. Victims often feel powerless and not in control of the events happening around them. For that reason, it's important to include them in the process. Providing them with information about what will happen and the expected course of events can help to empower victims and decrease anxiety.

Some victims may ask you not to make a report. This is natural, as they may fear consequences from the perpetrator or may simply fear upsetting the family dynamic. Though a reaction such as this is understandable, you should not let this influence your decision to make the call. You can, however, explain your reasoning to the child, providing them with details about what will happen and letting them know that you will ensure their safety no matter what.

Should I confront the abuser?

It is not particularly useful to confront a perpetrator of child sexual abuse. Your primary concern should be the child's safety, extricating them from the abusive situation, and taking the matter to the proper authorities. Keep in mind that perpetrators are skilled at normalizing situations and allaying fears. They may try to convince you that it wasn't what it looked like and that it's not as bad as it seems, or they may make promises that it will never happen again. They may even threaten you or draw attention to what the consequences may look like for the whole family. For these and other reasons, confrontation with the abuser is not recommended.

But what if the suspected perpetrator is a nice guy or someone I know and love?

Remember that abusers can be anyone, even "nice guys" who you would never believe could harm a child. A couple of years ago, we were regularly sending a team of our students to a prison in Pennsylvania to interview sex offenders. Back at our lab meeting on Monday mornings, we'd ask students how the week had gone and what their impressions were. Almost unfailingly, we would hear from students that they were surprised to find some of the offenders to be "really nice guys." One bonded with an offender over a shared love of the Rolling Stones. As should be clear from reading this book, offenders aren't always the creepy strangers we have in our minds. Often, they are people quite like us who we share an interest in music with or who simply seem to be people who wouldn't be capable of this kind of thing. They can be our family and friends—and no one wants to believe that someone we like could do something like abusing a child.

If there is one thing we've learned through the years, it's that sexual abuse can happen anywhere, including small towns, wealthy suburbs, and big cities. It happens in homes, it happens in schools, and it happens in plenty of places where we feel safe. Abuse can also be perpetrated by anyone—whether a father, uncle, trusted neighbor, babysitter, pediatrician, teacher, or priest. While we can't go through life distrusting everyone and constantly fearing for our children's safety, we do need to avoid the "it can't happen here" type of thinking that led earlier generations to ignore warning signs of abuse.

In Chapter 8, we introduced the concept of grooming, which generally refers to the building of trust with a child to set the stage for abuse. But grooming happens not just with the child, but also with the family and community. Offenders may use deliberate tactics to build the trust of family members so that they get time alone with the child or so that no one believes that they would be the type to do this. Children seldom lie about abuse, so if you are finding yourself believing the account of the perpetrator over that of the child, remember that you may have been groomed yourself.

Sometimes people face conflicts in reporting suspected abuse, especially when the abuser is part of a family. This type of report could cause major disruption to the family, even leading to a perpetrator facing charges and a child being taken from the home. But it is important that this fear of rocking the boat not come before the safety of a child.

What if I'm not sure about the abuse?

If in doubt, report it. Given that offenders work hard to conceal their abuse and may, if questioned, provide justifications—often reasonable sounding enough—for their behavior, it's not unusual to question whether what we are seeing is indeed abuse. The good news is that you don't have to make this decision! Child Protective Services (CPS) hotlines exist for this reason to take calls and do the work of substantiating whether abuse is occurring. Remember that your decision to report can have enormous impact in the life of a child. Sexual abuse can have serious and long-ranging effects. Remember that reporting suspected abuse does not require you to be certain that it is abuse. Hotlines exist to help you through this, and CPS will conduct their own investigation. You are only asked to report what you know, not to be 100 percent certain that abuse has happened.

Who should I contact if I suspect abuse?

You can call the police or CPS in your state or province. You can also call the helpline **1-888-PREVENT** provided by the StopItNow!

Organization, or **1-800-4-A-Child,** the ChildHelp National Child Abuse Hotline. These hotlines allow you to remain anonymous, can answer general questions about abuse and how the CPS hotlines work, and will connect you to resources in your area.

What will happen?

An investigation will be conducted. Typically, this involves someone (often a social worker) making a visit to the house, usually within a day of the report. The child and family members are usually interviewed privately. The child may be asked to complete a physical exam. After the evidence is gathered, a determination is made. The abuse report will either be considered substantiated or unfounded. An unfounded determination doesn't necessarily mean that no abuse occurred; it simply means that there was not sufficient evidence to make that determination at the time.

If CPS does not substantiate abuse but you believe or know it to be going on, you should continue to take action. If the child is in immediate danger, call the police or 911. You can also ask to speak to a supervisor in your local Child Protective Services office. And importantly, you should document anything you learn—photos, video, audio, and any additional type of evidence you may have. If the report is substantiated, the family may be referred to community or in-home services, and, in some cases, the child may be removed from the home. What happens in these cases usually depends on state policy, the severity of the abuse, whether the abuse was one-time or is ongoing, and the risk of future incidents.

Am I required to make a report?

Possibly, depending on your job. As discussed in Chapter 2, some people by nature of their profession are required by law to report suspected abuse. Teachers, social workers, doctors, nurses, psychologists, and others (depending on who is statutorily listed as a mandated reporter in your state) must call and report suspected abuse.

What if someone over the age of eighteen discloses abuse as a child?

Your concern should be twofold. First, finding out whether there may be another child presently at risk. If so, the ideal course of action is to encourage the person who disclosed the abuse to you to make a report. That person has the most information and, given their own abuse history, can provide details that might help social workers evaluate the current situation. Second, you should help the person who disclosed to you access any supportive services they might need. They may, or may not, want help. Your role is to listen, validate their experience, and empower them to make the best decisions for themselves. A person is not required in any way to report their own abuse, but should be encouraged to do so if risk to others is ongoing.

What should I do if I'm just in a bystander situation where someone looks uncomfortable?

It's also possible that you are a bystander to a situation where someone could be harmed. In these situations, we encourage you to act. Intervening in some way in the situation has the potential to stop an assault before it happens.

The Green Dot bystander intervention program has been gaining national attention due to its demonstrated success in reducing the incidence of sexual perpetration.[98, 99] Earlier in Chapter 10, we discussed how telling women to be careful (and to not go out alone at night or to practice self-defense)—while

---

98   Coker, A. L., B. S. Fisher, H. M. Bush, S. C. Swan, C. M. Williams, E. R. Clear, and S. DeGue. 2014. Evaluation of the Green Dot bystander intervention to reduce interpersonal violence among college students across three campuses. *Violence Against Women* 21(12): 1507–27. doi: 10.1177/1077801214545284.

99   Cook-Craig, P. G., P. H. Millspaugh, E. A. Recktenwald, N. C. Kelly, L. M. Hegge, A. L. Coker, and T. S. Pletcher. 2014. From empower to Green Dot: Successful strategies and lessons learned in developing comprehensive sexual violence primary prevention programming. Violence Against Women 20(10): 1162-78. doi: 10.1177/1077801214551286.

well-intentioned—inadvertently puts the blame of a sexual assault on them. The Green Dot program, which is used in many colleges and other organizations across the country, seeks to stop abuse by empowering the witnesses to those events to intervene in some manner. It is built on the idea that small steps by each and every one of us—whether by challenging cultural norms that support sexual violence or acting in some way to diffuse a high-risk situation—have the potential to whittle away at our sexual violence problem.

Box 18: State by State Numbers
to Call to Report Abuse and Neglect[100]

Alabama
dhr.alabama.gov/services/Child_Protective_Services
   /Abuse_Neglect_Reporting.aspx
Click on the website above for information on reporting or call
   Childhelp® (800-422-4453) for assistance.

Alaska
Toll-Free: (800) 478–4444
dhss.alaska.gov/ocs/Pages/default.aspx

Arizona
Toll-Free: (888) SOS-CHILD (888-767-2445)
dcs.az.gov/report-child-abuse

Arkansas
Toll-Free: (800) 482–5964
humanservices.arkansas.gov/dcfs/Pages/ChildProtective
   Services.aspx#Child

California
www.cdss.ca.gov/Reporting/Report-Abuse
Click on the website above for information on reporting or call
   Childhelp® (800-422-4453) for assistance.

Colorado
Local (toll): (844) 264-5437
co4kids.org

Connecticut
Toll-Free: (800) 842–2288
TDD: (800) 624–5518
www.ct.gov/dcf/cwp/view.asp?a=2556&Q=314388

---

100 US Department of Health and Human Services Administration for Children and Families. 2017. State Child Abuse and Neglect Reporting Numbers. Child Welfare and Information Gateway. Retrieved from https://www.childwelfare.gov/organizations/?CWIGFunctionsaction=rols:main.dspList&rolType=Custom&RS_ID=5.

Delaware
Toll-Free: (800) 292–9582
kids.delaware.gov/services/crisis.shtml

District of Columbia
Local (toll): (202) 671-SAFE (202-671-7233)
cfsa.dc.gov/service/report-child-abuse-and-neglect

Florida
Toll-Free: (800) 96-ABUSE (800-962-2873)
www.dcf.state.fl.us/abuse/

Georgia
Local (toll): (855)-GACHILD (855-422-4453) dfcs.dhs.georgia.
   gov/child-abuse-neglect

Hawaii
Local (toll): (808) 832–5300
humanservices.hawaii.gov/ssd/home/child-welfare-services/

Idaho
Local (toll): (855) 552-KIDS (5437)
TDD: (208) 332-7205
healthandwelfare.idaho.gov/Children/AbuseNeglect/ChildProtection
   ContactPhoneNumbers/tabid/475/Default.aspx

Illinois
Toll-Free: (800) 252–2873
Local (toll): (217) 524–2606
www.state.il.us/dcfs/child/index.shtml

Indiana
Toll-Free: (800) 800–5556
www.in.gov/dcs/2398.htm

Iowa
Toll-Free: (800) 362–2178
dhs.iowa.gov/report-abuse-and-fraud

Kansas
Toll-Free: (800) 922–5330
www.dcf.ks.gov/Pages/Report-Abuse-or-Neglect.aspx

Kentucky
Toll-Free: (877) 597–2331
chfs.ky.gov/dcbs/dpp/childsafety.htm

Louisiana
Toll-Free: (855) 452–5437
dss.louisiana.gov/index.cfm?md=pagebuilder&tmp
    =home&pid=109

Maine
Toll-Free: (800) 452–1999
TTY: (800) 963–9490
www.maine.gov/dhhs/ocfs/hotlines.htm

Maryland
dhr.maryland.gov/child-protective-services/reporting-suspected-
    child-abuse-or-neglect/local-offices/
Click on the website above for information on reporting or call
    Childhelp® (800-422-4453) for assistance.

Massachusetts
Toll-Free: (800) 792–5200
www.mass.gov/eohhs/gov/departments/dcf/child-abuse-neglect/

Michigan
Toll-Free: (855) 444–3911
Fax: (616) 977–1154
www.michigan.gov/mdhhs/0,5885,7-339-73971_7119-21208—
    ,00.html

Minnesota
mn.gov/dhs/people-we-serve/children-and-families/services
    /child-protection/contact-us/index.jsp
Click on the website above for information on reporting or call
    Childhelp® (800-422-4453) for assistance.

Mississippi
Toll-Free: (800) 222–8000
Local (toll): (601) 359–4368
www.mdcps.ms.gov

Missouri
Toll-Free: (800) 392–3738

dss.mo.gov/cd/can.htm

Montana
Toll-Free: (866) 820-5437
www.dphhs.mt.gov/cfsd/index.shtml

Nebraska
Toll-Free: (800) 652-1999
dhhs.ne.gov/children_family_services/Pages/children_family
 _services.aspx

Nevada
Toll-Free: (800) 992-5757
dcfs.nv.gov/Programs/CWS/CPS/CPS/

New Hampshire
Toll-Free: (800) 894-5533
Local (toll): (603) 271-6562
www.dhhs.state.nh.us/dcyf/cps/contact.htm

New Jersey
Toll-Free: (877) 652-2873
TDD: (800) 835-5510
TTY: (800) 835-5510
www.nj.gov/dcf/reporting/how/index.html

New Mexico
Toll-Free: (855) 333-7233
cyfd.org/child-abuse-neglect

New York
Toll-Free: (800) 342-3720
TDD: (800) 369-2437
Local (toll): (518) 474-8740
www.ocfs.state.ny.us/main/cps/

North Carolina
Local (toll): (919) 527-6340 www2.ncdhhs.gov/dss/local/index.
 htm

North Dakota
www.nd.gov/dhs/services/childfamily/cps/#reporting
Click on the website above for information on reporting or call
 Childhelp® (800-422-4453) for assistance.

Ohio
Toll-Free: (855) 642-4453
jfs.ohio.gov/ocf/reportchildabuseandneglect.stm

Oklahoma
Local (toll): (405) 521-2283
www.okdhs.org/services/cps/Pages/default.aspx

Oregon
Toll-Free: (855) 503-SAFE (7233)
www.oregon.gov/dhs/children/child-abuse/Pages/Reporting-
    Numbers.aspx

Pennsylvania
Toll-Free: (800) 932-0313
TDD: (866) 872-1677
www.dhs.pa.gov/citizens/reportabuse/index.htm#.
    Vr4FO032aM8

Puerto Rico
Toll-Free: (800) 981-8333
Local (toll): (787) 749-1333

Rhode Island
Toll-Free: (800) RI-CHILD (800-742-4453)
www.dcyf.ri.gov/child_welfare/index.php

South Carolina
Local (toll): (803) 898-7318
dss.sc.gov/abuseneglect/report-child-abuse-and-neglect/

South Dakota
Local (toll): (877) 244-0864
dss.sc.gov/abuseneglect/report-child-abuse-and-neglect/

Tennessee
Toll-Free: (877) 237-0004
www.tn.gov/dcs/article/report-child-abuse

Texas
Toll-Free: (800) 252-5400
www.dfps.state.tx.us/Contact_Us/report_abuse.asp

US Virgin Islands
www.dhs.gov.vi/contact/index.html

Utah
Toll-Free: (855) 323-3237
dcfs.utah.gov/services/preventabuse/

Vermont
After hours: (800) 649-5285
dcf.vermont.gov/protection/reporting

Virginia
Toll-Free: (800) 552-7096
Local (toll): (804) 786-8536
www.dss.virginia.gov/family/cps/index.cgi

Washington
Toll-Free: (866) END-HARM (866-363-4276)
Toll-Free: (800) 562-5624
TTY: (800) 624-6186
www1.dshs.wa.gov/ca/safety/abuseReport.asp?2

West Virginia
Toll-Free: (800) 352-6513
www.wvdhhr.org/bcf/Pages/default.aspx

Wisconsin
dcf.wisconsin.gov/reportabuse
Click on the website above for information on reporting or call
    Childhelp® (800-422-4453) for assistance.

Wyoming
sites.google.com/a/wyo.gov/dfsweb/social-services/child-
    protective-services
Click on the website above for information on reporting or call
    Childhelp® (800-422-4453) for assistance.

CHAPTER 12

Ways to Help Your Community Stop Sexual Violence

We have now reached the last chapter in this book. Our aim was to provide you with data about the realities of sexual offending and show you how these dangers can be addressed and minimized in your child's life. Most of what we have shared has focused on what you—as an individual parent—can do to protect *your* children. However, that is only part of the story. As the proverb says, "It takes a village to raise a child"—and this includes sexual violence prevention. While there are many things we can do as parents on a micro level to keep our children safe, sexual violence is not so much an individual issue as it is a community and societal issue. In this chapter, we will show you how you can work with your community to decrease the risk for sexual violence for *all* children.

I am doing what I can as a parent, but what can my community do to keep my child safe?

Sexual violence is not a problem that happens in isolation. The Centers for Disease Control and Prevention (CDC) uses what is called the socio-ecological model (see Box 19) to understand sexual violence and how to prevent it. The prevention strategies we have discussed so far in this book mostly pertain to the Individual and Relationship levels: things that we can do with our child, or in our families, to prevent sexual violence. But sexual abuse does not happen in a vacuum—it is part of a larger problem.

As you can see from the diagram, sexual violence can also be prevented on the Community and Societal level. While changing societal values and norms is integral to making change, these types of changes can take a long time (sometimes an entire generation). For example, in our parents' generation, it may have been acceptable to call women "honey" or "sweetie" and perhaps even to pat them on the behind. Today, this is seen as sexualizing and demeaning and would constitute sexual harassment and even sexual assault. While this is a positive change, it took many years to happen, and some people still behave this way. Although attitudes and beliefs such as these may seem harmless, they support sexual violence. Marginalization, degradation, and oppression of a group leads to violence. If men believe that women are sexualized objects (which is how they are depicted in ads for Hooters and in the *Sports Illustrated Swim Suit Edition*), then what is the harm in treating them in a sexualized manner?

This social phenomenon was shown in the discussions of "locker room talk" during the leadup to the 2016 presidential election, when then-presidential candidate Donald J. Trump was recorded saying, "You know I'm automatically attracted to beautiful—I just start kissing them. It's like a magnet. Just kiss. I don't even wait. And then when you're a star they let you do it. You can do anything . . . grab them by the pussy. You can do anything." These comments ignited a fierce debate, and some individuals, including the presidential candidate himself, referred to his language as harmless "locker room banter," while others argued that this language was indicative of sexual assault. Because this type of talk, which many said happens in locker rooms across the country, is supposedly normal, the implication is that the talk itself—and the behaviors that are suggested—are in some way okay. Just like it is no longer okay to pat co-workers on the behind, these types of social norms must be changed if we want to get rid of sexual violence. Research shows that societies with more egalitarian beliefs toward women have lower incidences of sexual assault, while those cultures and societies with more patriarchal and machistic views have higher rates of sexual violence.[101] Words and beliefs do make a difference.

However, if we want to do something on a larger or more macroscale—but something that can still make a difference now—we can also look to start prevention initiatives in our communities. Before we determine what we can do in our communities, we have to define what we mean by *community*, as it has many meanings. Community can mean your neighborhood, cultural or religious community, child's school, town, city, or even state or province. All of these are communities—some are bigger, and some are smaller. Obviously, it is easier to organize a neighborhood or school of parents than an entire state or province, but all are possible, and all can have a role in keeping your child safe.

The biggest thing we can do as community members is to talk to one another. At the end of this book, we have compiled discussion questions that can be used to start conversations. However, conversations are only the first step. Once you gather your community, you will have to do a "needs assessment" to determine what is needed in your community. Each community is different and may require different levels of involvement and intervention. Once you decide what is needed, then you can work

---

101 World Health Organization. 2002. Chapter 6: Sexual Violence. In Krug, E. G., L .L. Dahlberg, J. A. Mercy, A. B. Zwi, and R. Lozano. (eds), *World report on violence and health* (pp. 149–181). Geneva: World Health Organization. Retrieved from http://www.who.int/violence_injury_prevention/violence/global_campaign/en/chap6.pdf

to address those needs. Ideas can include prevention initiatives such as education campaigns or working with at-risk youth. One study found that most sexual assaults of children took place in the after-school hours and over the summer, times when children may be unattended or in the care of others as their parents are at work.[102] Thus, developing after-school and summer camp programs for kids that would otherwise be unsupervised is a step towards decreasing risk of sexual abuse.

I want to do more—how do I do that?

First, you should be commended for your desire to get involved and make a difference. Every case of sexual abuse that is prevented makes a tremendous difference. Next, you want to get informed. Reading this book is a good first step. In addition to the information we have discussed in the chapters, we have provided a reading list of books and articles that can help you better understand the problem and possible solutions.

You should then define the community within which you want to participate (neighborhood, town, school, state/province). If you are new to this, it may be easier to make small steps and start with your immediate community (neighborhood or school). On the other hand, if nothing is currently being done in your immediate community, you may want to look to larger organizations on the state or provincial level that are already established—like RAINN (https://www.rainn.org/) or Prevent Child Abuse America (http://preventchildabuse.org/)—where you can learn how to get involved on a community level.

If you are not comfortable doing this on your own, recruit a partner, such as another parent, friend, or relative, who can

---

102 Colombino, N. 2016. Preventing sexual violence where it most often occurs: An investigation of the situational and structural components of child sexual abuse in residential settings. Unpublished dissertation.

accompany you on this journey. The more of us out there fighting to prevent sexual violence, the better!

How can I identify potential community partners?

The first place to start is identifying the leaders in your community. This may the president of your neighborhood association, the president of the PTO/PTA, the Girl or Boy Scout leader, religious or cultural leaders in your community, the school principal, or the mayor, among others. On the other hand, it may not be a formal leader at all, but rather another involved parent or even a high school student who is motivated to make a difference.

Reach out to these individuals and state that you are seeking them out because of their leadership role in the community. You will want to personalize your letter to them—see a sample letter in Box 20.

While your organization will likely grow as you become established and word gets out, you will want to have a core group with some kind of executive committee. Some of these core members may be there because they represent connections to the community or can provide resources, while others may be involved because they simply want to make a difference and contribute their time and dedication. Your organization may grow in form and scope depending upon this core group, but developing a mission statement is a great first step and will keep your group/ organization focused on the big picture.

People do not like talking about this topic, but I know it is important—how can I bring them to the table?

As we talked about in the overview of this book, sexual violence is not a topic many people are comfortable talking about. However, it is a topic people are interested in. *Law and Order: Special Victims Unit*, a show focused on sexual violence, has been on TV for eighteen years!

We have found that using statistics and the stories of those who have experienced sexual assault works to get people interested and talking. Because sexual violence can be a hard topic to discuss, many people still have a lot of misconceptions. Flyers and print materials such as those provided in the links in Box 21 can be used to get people's attention—sending these via social media or even traditional e-mail or snail mail may be enough to get some people talking. Another option would be to invite a guest speaker who has expertise in sexual violence prevention. Having experts to lead the discussion can be enough to get people in the room.

Sometimes it just involves us getting over our own fears and simply talking. In this book, we discuss how to overcome our fears and discomfort when speaking to our children, and the same principles can be applied to starting a conversation in the community. Sexual violence is something that will affect all of us at some level, and we all have the responsibility to do our part.

Okay, I got some people/groups together—so now what do we do?

First—hooray! This is a big first step. The next step is to decide what you want to do. The size of your community and the resources available to you will largely dictate your initial endeavors, but if you want to grow and develop your organization, the sky is the limit.

Good first steps are brainstorming what would be 1) ideal and 2) feasible to do in your community. While there may be little overlap between these two lists at the moment, you will see that as your organization grows and develops, what was once a dream is now feasible.

Here are some questions you can ask your group to get you going:

- Who do we want to target?

- What do we want to do?
- What resources are currently at our disposal/what resources do we think we can get?
- What has already been done? What has worked and what has not worked?
- How much time do we have to dedicate?
- What kind of buy-in do we have from other members of the community (i.e., will this be a hard or easy sell)
- How long will this take?

Once you get some of these things down on paper, you need to decide your plan of action: how to get from where you are to where you want to be. The good news about having a group is that each person will come with their own strengths—some may have connections, others are good with advertising or community outreach, and others are good at organization. Empowering people through their skills will help the group move forward and reach your goal.

Are there evidence-based prevention initiatives that we should know about?

Yes! There are some very exciting new initiatives that are being developed to prevent sexual violence. The best place to go to find out about what works is the CDC website. They conduct rigorous evaluations of programs to let the public know what works and what is promising. Currently in the "what works" domain are several programs that address prevention of dating violence and sexual harassment among middle school– and high school–aged boys and girls. The two programs that have demonstrated results are:

- **Safe Dates:** a program designed to prevent physical, emotional, and sexual abuse from starting in dating relationships, which targets male and female

students in the eighth and ninth grade: http://www.
violencepreventionworks.org/public/safe_dates.page.

- **Shifting Boundaries:** this program is designed to
  decrease dating violence and sexual harassment among
  teens. It targets male and female middle school students
  and is comprised of two parts. The first part is a six-
  session classroom-based course, which is then followed
  with school-wide rules to reinforce what has been used
  in the classroom: https://www.crimesolutions.gov/
  ProgramDetails.aspx?ID=226.

There is also one program that has been found to reduce sexual
violence perpetration behaviors among college men called **Real-
Consent** (http://www.jmir.org/2014/9/e203/). Several other programs are currently labeled as *promising* (meaning that they have
good preliminary results but need more research to show that
they really work). These include:

- **Green Dot:** a prevention program that promotes positive
  bystander behaviors and works to change social norms
  to decrease sexual and interpersonal violence: http://
  livethegreendot.com/.
- **Second Step: Student Success Through Prevention
  (SS:SSTP):** a school-based program targeting bullying,
  victimization, and other problem behaviors and that
  has been shown to reduce sexual violence: http://www
  .cfchildren.org/second-step/middle-school.
- **Coaching Boys into Men:** a dating violence prevention
  program that uses the relationship between athletic
  coaches and teenage boys to demonstrate prosocial
  behaviors in dating relationships and positive attitudes
  toward women with the goal of changing social norms
  and decreasing sexual and physical dating violence:

http://www.futureswithoutviolence.org/engaging-men/
coaching-boys-into-men/.

- **Bringing in the Bystander:** a bystander intervention program for college students (both male and female) designed to teach individuals how to get involved by speaking out against rape myths and sexist language, supporting victims, and knowing how to intervene in potentially dangerous situations: http://cola.unh.edu/prevention-innovations/bystander.

What kinds of resources are out there for community groups?

There are many resources available to community groups that are getting started. Many organizations have developed online trainings, guides, and podcasts that can be accessed free of charge. There are leadership conferences and lists of speakers available at your disposal. Depending on your resources, it may even be feasible for your group to hire someone to help you develop your organization. These resources may not necessarily be specific to sexual violence prevention (while some may be). See Box 22 for a list of possible resources to help your community groups.

If this is a societal level problem—how can working within my community make a difference?

Sexual abuse is indeed a societal problem, but every step taken at every level makes a difference. Many large-scale societal problems have been changed by grassroots efforts. The more each and every one of us does our part, the larger the movement will grow to the point where we do see bigger societal change.

What are the next steps to stopping sexual violence?

You have read this book—that is a huge first step. We hope that we have now got you thinking about these issues and how they relate to keeping your own children and your community safer from sexual violence. Working with your families on an individual and relational level, as well as on a community level, is extremely important to preventing sexual violence. However, as long as there is a tacit societal acceptance of these behaviors and actions, the larger problem will persist. We all need to work together to change social norms supportive of sexual violence. We hope that this book has given you tangible advice and tips that you as a parent can follow to keep your own children safer. Additionally, we hope we have empowered you with the knowledge and skills so that we can all work together to make change!

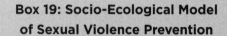

Box 19: Socio-Ecological Model of Sexual Violence Prevention

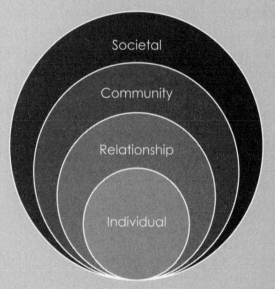

Societal

Community

Relationship

Individual

Based upon CDC Social-Ecological Model,
www.cdc.gov/violenceprevention/overview/social-ecologicalmodel.html

Box 20: Sample Letter

Hi, my name is X, and I want to prevent sexual violence in our community by developing a working group of community members. I am reaching out to you because of your role in Y. As you are a leader in our community, I would love for you to be involved as it is clear that you are interested in X and are working to make our community safer for everyone. Would you be interested in serving as a member of this working group?

Box 21: Sample Flyers and Print Materials

www.pinterest.com/pin/247135098274579819/

www.nsvrc.org/sites/default/files/publications_nsvrc
_factsheet_media-packet_statistics-about-sexual-violence_0.pdf

www.nsvrc.org/publications/nsvrc-publications-sexual-
assault-awareness-month/saam-2015-poster

www.rainn.org/print-materials

Box 22

Resources for Community Groups: resources.depaul.edu/abcd-
institute/about/Pages/default.aspx

Principles of Effective Prevention Programs: www.mentoring.org
/old-downloads/mentoring_4.pdf

9 Principles of Effective Prevention Programs: wiki.preventconnect
.org/Nine+Principles+of+Effective+Prevention+Programs

Protecting Students from Sexual Assault: www.justice.gov/ovw
/protecting-students-sexual-assault

Discussion Questions

We showed you the following diagram in Chapter 12 about the different levels of sexual violence prevention. In this discussion question section, we are going to highlight some important things you can ask to start the conversation on sexual violence prevention at each level.

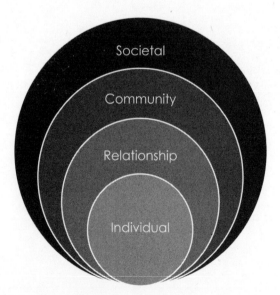

Based upon CDC Social-Ecological Model,
www.cdc.gov/violenceprevention/overview/social-ecologicalmodel.html

Individual Level:

1. Are the data presented in this book consistent with my ideas about sexual offenses and sexual offenders? What, if any, misconceptions did I have? Where might these misconceptions have come from?
2. Do I talk to my children about their bodies and healthy sexuality? Have I had this conversation more than once?
   a. If not—why not?
3. Have I talked to my children about sexual violence prevention?
   a. If not—why not? What is standing in my way?
4. Do I model gender equality and respect for both men and women? In what ways might I fall short of this goal? Is there room for improvement?

Relationship Level:

1. Do we model healthy relationships in our home? Is there room for improvement and, if so, in what ways?
2. Do I show respect to my partner and does my partner show respect to me? In what ways can we work to further model respect for others in our home?
3. Do our family values reflect an attitude of respect for both men and women? Are we equals in our relationship?
4. What are the values of my children's friends and their families?
5. Are my children respectful in their relationships with others? Do they seek consent from others or try to coerce others into doing things they don't want to?

Community Level:

1. What is the school in your community doing, if anything, to teach young children about sexual violence prevention? If there is no programming, is there someone you can talk to who might facilitate this? If there is programming, do you know what it entails?
2. What kind of discussions of healthy sexuality are the children getting in school or in their after-school activities?
3. Are our teens learning about healthy relationships and how to prevent sexual violence?
4. Do people in our community know about bystander intervention programs?
5. What is being done outside of the school to prevent sexual violence?
6. Who are the leaders in our community who could address issues related to sexual violence prevention?

Societal Level:

1. What is being done to challenge attitudes that support sexual violence? How can we each do more?
2. What policies are in place to prevent sexual violence? Discuss policies in your city or state and whether these policies are likely to have an impact on sexual violence.
3. What societal norms do we hold that promote sexual violence? Think of any examples—positive or negative—you may have heard over the past month or so that reflect how society views sexuality and sexual violence.

Index